MW00563227

Violence of Mind

Preparation for Extreme Violence

Varg Freeborn
www.violenceofmind.com
https://www.patreon.com/ViolenceofMind

Editing by
Lauren Bechtel

Cover Art and Design by
Lorin Michki

Table of Contents

Preface

Information is everywhere. I am not claiming to have the *one true way*, nor am I claiming that all the information in this work was created by me. Humans have been sharing, synthesizing and creating new forms of information since we have learned to communicate. In the fight training world, this sharing community is smaller and more specialized. Everything we have in skills, techniques, procedures and tactics has been created, tested, refined, and handed down so that the process starts all over again. For thousands of years, in the warrior culture, battles, wars and contests in sport fighting have boiled off the bad and handed down the effective. It is how we continually grow and develop in the martial disciplines.

Born from my experiences, this book is my endeavor to share my personal views, beliefs and methodologies about violence and training. You will find that those experiences are quite unique and, while uncommon for a fighting and tactics instructor, absolutely relevant to the subject matter. Trying to break down the conditioning that creates the calm, decisive, steely-eyed apex fighter and pass it on to the inexperienced is the mystery code everyone is trying to unlock in the higher levels of the training world. When we go into the gym or on the range, we should be working the fundamentals. The rest of the time, we need to be building the mindset. This is the first task I will try to deliver in this book.

I have tried to cite and credit the proper sources when I've felt the need to use concepts or quotes from others. Thank you. I hope I can pay that forward someday and have the same effect on others that they have had on my life and my career. Those of you who have influenced me, thank you. I am sure you will see your legacy here, as I have seen my own live through my students' words as well.

To be clear, in no way do I hold this book as an exhaustive work. This book is intended to share information from my own unique perspective and meant to be an introduction. Each section in this book could be its own book (if not volumes). The sheer scope of this work renders it to be an excellent introduction into violence mindset and fight training.

I'd also like to thank all of you fuckers who kicked the shit out of me, and the few who tried to kill me, over the years. The training I received from you tops anything money could ever buy.

I'm still here.

About this book

Before I began work on this book, I made it a rule not to get extremely technical with scientific terms and big words. I want this to be digestible to everyone. Which sounds better:

- "Our primary objective is to gain a kinesthetic awareness of where our bipedal foundation is as we transition dynamically through the transverse and sagittal planes so as to maintain maximum musculoskeletal leverage and stability"

  OR:

- We need to understand that where we place our feet and how we move at the waist will have a huge effect on how stable we are

I'm assuming option two is preferable. It's not a "dynamic critical stress event" or whatever. It's a fight. Let's speak directly and simply. It's hard enough to grasp and internalize all of the concepts involved with fight training without all of the big technical jargon getting in the way (and let's hope that particular marketing trend dies a rapid and public death soon). It's also important to point out that this book will not be about "what" to train as much as it is about "how" to train, and even more specifically how to think.

The mindset of fighting and the structure of training protocol are the first and most important tasks to tackle when making the decision to train for defensive gun fighting, or any kind of violent fighting. Based on my experience, I view this as a priority, because skipping these first steps is the most common mistake in the training world. This book will serve as an *introduction* to my concepts and methods, which will all be expanded on in my classes, future works and online coursework. Just remember, it's impossible to put it all down in one place, *so there is more behind every thought within these pages.*

Everyone loves to just jump right in and start shooting (or learning submissions), without giving much thought to the violence this is about. There may be a few drills or techniques explained here, but what I am really trying to accomplish is to lay the groundwork for everything that you will train, from here forward. To understand what we are doing, why we are doing it, who we are doing it to, and when we should do it. I hope you will agree that these should be accomplished before you learn "how" to do it. The goal is to be a fighter that is properly oriented and conditioned, able to operate with a controlled mindset in chaos, while being completely focused on a clearly defined mission.

I am also going to give you a clear look into the violent criminal mind, a topic which I am intimately acquainted with. After literally growing up in extreme criminal violence, and then having spent two decades in and around martial arts, firearms and other "self-defense" training, I am convinced that few truly know the enemy or understand what they must do to be able to meet him head-on someday. Hopefully, I can begin to rectify that here.

Most of all, I've simply attempted to write the book that I wish I could have found many years ago when I was desperately looking for guidance on this subject. I hope it delivers at least some tangible advantages to all the good guys, and girls, out there. My command of the language is not particularly profound, so there will be mistakes here. My editor, Lauren, did a phenomenal job, mostly just wrestling with me over making changes to my book. Whatever is incorrect is undoubtedly my fault, probably left at my insistence. I like to write with the same voice that I speak. My goal was not to write a grammatically perfect book, or a best-seller for that matter. My simple goal here is to share my first-hand experience with extreme criminal violence and violence preparedness in an introductory level text that is written so the average person can begin to understand how violence works in our society. My mission in this business is to teach people how to be professionals with the tools and knowledge of violence.

WHAT DO I KNOW ABOUT VIOLENCE ANYWAY?

I have been in a few hundred fights. I have put close to 30 holes in other men, and I've had a few put into me. I endured more beatings before age 10 than most of you would ever receive in a lifetime. I was charged, at one point, with Attempted Aggravated Murder for stabbing a man 23 times...

To receive the words that will follow in this book as viable information, you will need to have some belief in my legitimacy and knowledge. After all, the self-defense world is full of *experts who have never actually done the thing they are experts in*. That is, they have not actually participated in real, deadly violence. So, right out of the gate, let's establish who I am and what it means when I think something is important in fighting or training. Before I descend into those dark pits of my memories, let me be clear that my sole motivation in life is to add value to the world through helping others. Therefore, I exist, it is what motivates me and brings me reward. Violence education is merely one expression of that. This book is not going to be a biography and there is an awful lot I will purposely leave out of my story, but it is important to understand *why* I come to the conclusions that I do about fighting and training. When I am writing, talking or on the range teaching about self-defense against the violent criminal, I know with confidence that I am firmly planted in my lane, having spent 25 years living and participating in the violent criminal underworld.

The meat and potatoes of this work will be the training information contained in the following chapters. I built my training business and reputation completely off of my content and until the end of 2016 I never told any extensive personal story from my past in any class. I wanted my teaching and material to succeed on its own merit, not because students liked my war stories from the streets, or because they wanted to be attached to some *badassery*. I've attended classes where the instructors pretty much tell their own war stories for a good portion of the class, and it's disappointing to say the least. Students aren't paying for story-time; they're paying for a solution to a problem. That problem is a need for advantages in the fight against the bad guy.

As I reluctantly share a small piece of my history, please don't lose sight of the fact that *war stories* can be a distraction from the material being taught. I can't deny I have downplayed my past to a good degree. This book is part of my legacy, and I don't want more than needs to be known immortalized in it. However, this groundwork is necessary before we move on to the purpose we are here for: training for the fight.

I was born to a 16-year-old, single teenage mom. Her own mother had died 12 years before that, and my grandfather was raising his eight kids by himself. Since he worked in the steel mill and was gone all the time, the kids raised themselves. They didn't do a very good job of it. My uncles were drug dealers, convicts, gang members and small-time mob guys. My aunts were drug addicts and alcoholics. The household was extremely violent. My young mother tried pretty hard and worked several jobs. Unfortunately, this left me to the mercy of the rest of the household. Sadly, she thought she was doing the right thing to get us out of there and to a better atmosphere, when in reality I was being conditioned in a way that would seal my fate, to a large degree, forever.

Our house was a drug house. With so many aunts and uncles all under the age of 30, the house was a hangout for all of their friends. That was a lot of criminals under one roof every single day. Drugs and alcohol were daily props, and all of the bad that comes with that. This pretty much created the atmosphere I grew up in. Daily parties, sex, violence, friends and family dying or going to prison; I was never a fan of rap but looking back retrospectively, if you listen to any 2Pac song and just imagine a white version of that life and you pretty much have the correct mental image of what life was like in the late 80's and early 90's for some of us.

To give just one example, I was 6 years old the first time I nearly became a murder victim. This is a question I often ask when someone begins to expound about how much they know about violence, "How old were you the first time you almost became a murder victim?" For me it was 6, and it was just the beginning. The memories of how it began are long gone, but I'll never forget the moments of terror during the event. There was a drug-fueled knife attack in our house. My family members were being stabbed, but my aunt and mother had managed to get the three of us into grandpa's bedroom and put his big blue tool chest in front of the door. Thank God it was an inward swinging door (push door!). What happened next is something I will never forget. The hollow core door began to split, and the knife blade was visibly stabbing through. The attacker was shouting, "I'm going to kill all of you motherfuckers! Especially that little bastard in there with you; I'm going to chop him up into little pieces!"

He was referring to me. I'll never forget that feeling of being convinced that I was about to die in the most horrendous way possible. Chopped into little pieces while still alive. Right about that time, one of my uncles came home and a vicious fight took place. Of course, it was a long time before I was allowed out of the bedroom, but I could hear it and I was scared senseless for my uncle. When they finally allowed us out of the bedroom, there was no sign of the attacker or my uncle. Blood was everywhere, and I distinctly remember it being all over the kitchen cupboards. No one ever spoke of that event again. To this day, I am the only one who spoke of it, and only now because the participants have all passed away.

I know to most this sounds terribly traumatic and horrible. It was. What is different for me, and people who grow up like I did, is that it is just one of many, many experiences like this. It is worth mentioning that very early in life my young brain reached two very important conclusions:

- There are people who will kill the fuck out of you for no good reason.

- Violence DOES solve problems, specifically problems like that (and the worse it is, the more chance there is that violence is the *only* thing that will solve it.)

Unfortunately, my orientation and paradigm would continually be shaped by events like this for the next 19 years. My uncle Rosco ended up doing time in the penitentiary in El Paso. My uncle Tom did federal time in Kentucky. My uncle Kenny, who rode with the largest 1% gang in the nation, was murdered in Los Angeles. They beat him at his home, as evidenced by the blood on his couch, and took him to an orchard where they dragged him with a vehicle and then shot him execution style three times in the head with a .38 Special. He was still alive when they found him, but he died a few hours later in the hospital. My grandfather was an incredibly strong and cursed man. He buried his wife and over half of his children before he passed from this earth.

I also found my uncle Tom dead on the floor from OxyContin. I had saved this particular uncle more than once from an overdose, including one time that he aspirated vomit into his lungs after eating half of a pineapple turnover cake and overdosing on opiates. Saving each other and patching up holes was something we got a lot of experience doing. That last time though, no one was there to save him. A man who I considered one of the toughest and strongest men ever to live, a former street fighter and very high-level martial artist, was on the floor in front of me purple and swollen. Lifeless. I had been sent into the apartment by my mother, and I had to go back out and give her the news that her last brother was now dead. She didn't take it well and responded with denial, which of course I had to work her through amidst the screams and collapsing on the sidewalk in front of the apartments.

This is a scene that we knew all too well in our family. It extended to my friends and their families as well. When we were teenagers, one of my best friends lost his dad to family violence. Apparently, his dad and his uncle were arguing about who was going to drive the truck to the store to get more beer. It ended with the uncle shooting his own brother with a rifle in the front yard. My friend lost his dad to domestic violence. Another friend's mom shot his dad, but he lived. In another episode, one of my very closest friends, Patrick, was found floating in a local lake with a few bullet holes in his head. I was away when this happened, and no one was ever arrested for it.

This was in the late 1980's to early 1990's in Youngstown, years remembered for their carnage and bloodletting. And we were right in the middle of all of it. Like most violence, if you were not involved in the drug trade or from that demographic you were pretty much safe and probably remember a different version. But for those of us kids born into it, we had no choice but to--one way or another--be a part of it.

Around 10 years old, my mother married, and my dad adopted me. He turned out to be a drunk and a drug addict too. He had a terrible temper and gave me drunk beatings from time to time, often choking me until I thought I would die for sure. One day I had decided I would end that problem with the answer that I knew very well. I was waiting for him with an aluminum ball bat. He came into my room in a drunken rage and I rung his fucking bell like Reggie Jackson. He ended up deaf in his left ear for the rest of his life, and he never put a hand on me again.

That is an extremely shallow glossing over of what my childhood was like growing up. The details of my life are not important. I am conveying just enough to firmly establish my perspective as a violence educator. I spent my teenage years fighting and engaging in the usual behavior for someone from my demographic. My family was involved heavily in the illicit drug business. I promise you, this was the shit that they make movies about. It's amazing I survived the fights, weapons, stabbings, shootings, bar fights (yes, we were drinking and fighting in bars as teenagers), car wrecks, drugs, drug deals and alcohol. I never set foot inside of a high school. I never went to a prom, or attended a high school ball game. We mostly just got bent and fought. I was raised by wolves, and a quite nasty pack of them at that. I was a young wolf.

By 18 I had seen more death, cracked more heads and spilled more blood than most average "professionals" will do in their entire careers. But it wasn't over yet. When I was 18 my life took a dramatic turn, after which I would never be the same. As bad as it had been up until then, a hard road was only beginning...

A somewhat detailed version of the next set of events will now be described since it is important for some of the information that will later be discussed in this book. This is the first time I have told this story publicly in this detail, outside of private legal documents between my attorney and I.

I was approached by a guy much larger and older than I was because he was dating an ex-girlfriend and she apparently wanted me back. When I found out about him I parted ways with her because I just wasn't interested in fighting over her. It was too late, he had become fixated on me and our fates were sealed already. He pursued me for several months, vandalized my 1977 LTD to the point it had to be scrapped, and eventually attacked me in a driveway one night. We fought pretty hard, but I was out of shape and didn't have the conditioning to do any real damage on a much larger opponent.

I began to make a paper trail and reported the attack to the police, in response to which the police did absolutely nothing. Three days later, I was at a get-together in the neighborhood and here he came, at 1:30AM, with 2 friends. He was incredibly drunk, and fucking jacked up beyond all reasoning. After unsuccessfully attempting to get me to leave with him for an hour (thinking they would take me off somewhere alone), he finally began to escalate steadily. Remember, this was 1993, cell phones weren't a thing and this house didn't even have a landline. I also did not have a car with me that night. People I personally knew were getting routinely killed or maimed during this time frame, *knowledge that was an important part of my orientation and decision-making process*. I was trapped, and outnumbered.

He pursued me within the house, making threats about killing me, boasting about his (largely imaginary) mob ties, and really working himself into a rage. I repeatedly voiced for him to leave me alone. It didn't work. At some point, I noticed his two friends go outside and back the car up to the back door of the house. Around the same time, he begins pushing me from the front room to the rear of the home. I very loudly voiced warning after warning to him to not engage me. After all, I had been doing this violence thing for quite a few years now and if you made me fear for my life, I was very confident that no matter what, I would walk out of that room in the end. He didn't listen. I had been taken and held against my will before, so that car parked right outside the back door weighed heavily on my mind.

When I reached the rear room, where the back door was located, there was nowhere else to go. With three of them looming around me or close by waiting, I was in trouble. At age 18 I was just a 5'7" 130lbs kid soak and wet. I knew I didn't have the power or stamina to deal with what was at least 500 lbs. of angry dudes. He reached in to choke me, and I drew my blade up and stabbed him in his chest. He attacked more angrily than ever, and I went to work on him.

I have no clue how long the grappling, punching and stabbing went on. I counter-attacked until he quit attacking, which left him with holes in his chest, face, both sides of his neck, and his back. During the most intense grappling he was in extremely close trying to take me down, and I was reaching over him hitting him in the back with the 5" blade. His jugular was lacerated, his internal artery in his neck was lacerated, one lung was punctured, and he was in pneumothorax. In the end, he slid down the front of my body, leaving me completely soaked in his blood, and slumped rearward onto the floor, face up, and leaking out of over 20 holes.

When he slumped backwards, bleeding like nothing I had ever seen before, he looked up at me and gurgled out two words. Just two words he spoke. What do you think he said?

"I'm sorry."

The motherfucker looked up at me and said, "I'm sorry".

What. The. Fuck.

Apparently, remorse is a quality that comes to the surface as one lay at death's door.

Of course, I was fully convinced that I had just killed him and that he would be dead very soon. I also knew that I had 8 witnesses and 2 of his friends to deal with still. While they were very irate and freaking out, the two friends did not approach me. I stated my intention to walk outside and wait for police. And so, I did, and I went straight to jail. Later that night I was informed that somehow, amazingly, he did not die, and I would be charged with *attempted aggravated murder.*

I was now facing 25 years in prison.

In the months leading up to that night, and during that night, he was a real *tough guy.* Constant posturing, pursuing, stalking and harassing me. In court, however, he magically became this pitiful *victim,* and was "oh so stricken" by his wounds and his poor life was impacted forever, and on and on ad nauseum. Gone was the killer, the "mafia guy." In his place was the momma's boy, the good kid who just wanted to stop at a house to use the restroom that night. (Remember this for later, when I talk about the pitfalls of court.)

So how did it turn out? Well, he came to court and admitted a few key things. First, he openly admitted in court that he had absolutely pre-planned this attack on me. Yes, he said that, and I still have the transcripts. The judge couldn't believe his fucking ears and actually asked him to clarify it, to which he responded, "yeah, I was waiting for Freeborn to turn 18 so I could put my hands on him; so, I could get him." He also openly admitted that he had been drinking beer and Wild Turkey whiskey for 5 hours prior to the attack, and that he had went 15 miles out of his way to find me that night.

With these admissions, you would think I stood a pretty good chance at claiming self-defense, right? Wrong. There was no trial. Just to reach a plea bargain cost $8000, which luckily the entirety of my family was able to scrape together. A jury trial would have cost a minimum of another $20,000 to $40,000 and there was no fucking way anyone or anything in my life was going to produce that much money. The judge was not understanding to the fact that what I did was sheer brutality. *Stabbing someone a few dozen times just is not socially acceptable.* The court believed I went above and beyond "reasonable force in self-defense". So, as a 130lbs white teenage kid, I was sent to the penitentiary for a sentence of 2 to 5 years. I did the whole 5. From 19 to 24, I didn't see the outside world, and I became a man through fire.

As I already mentioned, this book is not the place to story tell so unfortunately you are not going to read about all of my adventures under the care of the state. It was eventful, to say the least. Remember, this was the 90's, so all of the guys who were doing the killing and carnage out there on the streets during one of the most violent eras we've had, were all now in one place. And so was I. I once did 75 days straight in "the hole", a small 7'x6'x7' metal isolation cell, for *suspicion* of stabbing another inmate. It was common for inmates not to snitch, so if a guard didn't witness it, it was probable that the inmates would wait to handle business on their own. In other words, revenge was a thing. Quite a few fights happened. I watched a few bodies go out under the sheet, and watched even more grown men lose their souls in other, arguably worse, ways. Many were kids just like me but unfortunately for them, they were not fighters. They suffered terribly.

I also used that time to develop myself in every way. I learned about fitness and working out. I hit the weight pile outside--no matter rain, shine or snow--and gained 50 lbs. of muscle. In fact, my very first "gym job" was being assigned to the prison gym and weight pile for clean-up and maintenance (which makes me laugh when I hear someone say they came up in "rough" gyms). I read books voraciously on every subject from religion and philosophy to politics and psychology. At some point I realized that I had reached the end of the glorification of my own violence. I had survived it all, and to go any further would be just repeating things I had already conquered until my luck ran out and I was either killed or locked up for good. I wanted something more.

I was released from prison in 1999, and I have never had a brush with the law since then. In fact, it's the only charge on my record. I moved to a new town far away from everyone I had known, and lived in an abandoned apartment with no electricity wired into it for almost two years. I worked a 40-hour job and went to vocational college 20 hours a week. For the first 6 months I lived out of a cooler. After that the nice old lady next door allowed me to run a single extension cord over. I've worked every day since then. By age 42, each year I claw my way up just a little higher, despite being legitimately road blocked over and over by a now 20 plus year old label.

I petitioned the court for a restoration of my rights upon review of my case. That restoration was granted, and I am a whole person outside of that label, able to vote, sit on a jury, hold public office and own and possess firearms as allowed by state and federal law. I can pass a NICS check. I was even granted certification to carry a pistol on security duty by the Attorney General of the State of Ohio. I am quite fortunate, and I still have to be very, very careful.

I was raised by wolves. I have been in a few hundred fights. Probably a dozen (or more) involved lethal-level force. I suffered extreme beatings as a kid. I've put dozens of holes in other men and have had a few put into me. I survived and thrived for 5 years in prison, the place I was sent to when I was a skinny white teenage kid, the house of wolves. I'm always skeptical of guys who claim the *badass* criminal background yet have no thoroughbred papers to prove it. I have those stories too: being interviewed for "suspicion" of racketeering, interviewed by the prison officials for "suspicion" of gang activity, pursued by the ATF for "suspicion" of weapons violations, interviewed (and locked in the hole for 75 days) for "suspicion" of stabbing another inmate...and some of those things I was suspected of were not even remotely true. So, I know on a personal level how much bullshit exists inside the "criminal" element. But I have legitimate release papers and documentation of the violence, that was true. As did the members of my family that raised me. Just like in other communities, there is a pedigree in this business.

After those violent years were behind me, I still needed a place for that part of me to go, so I moved into sanctioned fighting in the dojos and gyms. I trained in martial arts like BJJ, and boxing. I was fortunate to train under Ace Miller's staff in Knoxville for a brief time, and was also (much earlier) heavily influenced by Terry Garrett, a 6th Dan of Okinawan Shoin Ryu. I became a certified personal trainer and worked full-time training adults for several years. When my weapons restoration came through, I immediately began teaching law-abiding citizens and local law enforcement how to fight violent criminals with firearms.

I have also been fortunate enough to have trained with some of the best gunfighters in the world. I've trained under, and worked for, national level SWAT trainers, U.S. special forces veterans, Russian spetsnaz combat instructors, and many more. My work in the defense industry has granted me access to closed law enforcement training like breaching, executive protection and shoothouse courses for LE/mil only. I hold certifications to teach SWAT level full-team CQB, and have been approached to train at tactical officers training events. I continue my training with the best of the best and try to get at least 300 to 400 hours as a student in *per year.*

Through all my experiences on both sides of the tracks, I have accumulated the widest range of violence experience and training that I have ever heard of anyone having for the narrow lane of civilian criminal violence. Through all of this bloody conflict and high-level training, *orientation and conditioning* emerged as the most important components to have. Weapons and fighting skills only make up 20% of a fighter's capability. The other 80% is determined by what takes place in the mind.

These are arbitrary numbers, but I stand behind the ratio of importance. I learned that my orientation, my mindset, to the situation I was facing, was the single most deciding factor on whether I would win or lose. Sometimes that loss would have meant death, so this was undeniably important to me. I learned that skills without the conditioning to deliver those skills with strength, speed and endurance, are useless skills in a fight.

Later through fitness and fighting I began training other people. At the time of this writing, I have been training adults in one form or another for 15 years now. I found both my joy and my own growth in helping others achieve their goals. This naturally developed into helping them identify their goals, and then reach them. I spent several years as a certified professional fitness trainer, a career which I enjoyed immensely and was successful enough in to work full-time across several states.

Eventually that morphed into fight conditioning, fight training, gun fighting and, at a more mature level, violence education. Through all of this, the greatest adversary I have found in others and myself has been: the self. I have been the greatest adversary between me and my goals, just as you are to your goals. I added other positive learning experiences into my repertoire of knowledge to help overcome this and other obstacles in both my own path and in helping others on their paths as well.

In college I majored in sociology and completed all the coursework for the major, but not the general education requirements. I wasn't interested in spending $3000 multiple times to learn the history of art, or film, or some other horse-shit, useless subject. (90% of college is a scam, but that's another story). Having the unique set of experiences, I had coming into college, learning group and organizational behavior theory and statistics was quite interesting. It gave me an advantage over the individuals who filled the classrooms who had never experienced much in life. This included the professors, who generally went from mom and dad's house, to college, and just never left college.

I honestly learned exponentially more on my own. But the theories learned there meant something to me. I could reverse engineer situations and experiences and apply the learning immediately in retrospect. I began to understand the critical importance that culture and individual orientation hold in the framework of everything we do and every decision we make, both in fighting and in daily life. Culture shapes your decisions for how you will respond to violence, love, transactions...every life decision is drafted with the pallet of culture. However, culture is only one component of those filters. How we are conditioned and what our orientation filters are dictate how we see ourselves and the events that affect us.

I also worked for a criminal defense attorney for a little while as an assistant, which started as my internship in college. My job was to examine case law and propose arguments for the attorney with cited case law. After having spent years in a law library, and having fought the system to gain my own rights back on both a state and federal level, I had become very law savvy. The attorney would routinely tell me that I was "the most law savvy non-lawyer" he'd ever known.

This gave me an opportunity to see the judicial system from the inside, again yet another experience that I have literally been on both sides of. My conclusion, from all of my extensive experience with the judicial system, is that you only have the rights that you can afford to pay an attorney to defend. That attorney used to say, "the law has nothing to do with justice, and justice has nothing to do with truth." He was *so* honest about that. You may get lucky with a judge or a public defender, but in most cases if you don't have money you will go down in some capacity. I will speak more on this in later chapters.

Through these experiences, and having helped literally hundreds and hundreds of people grow on a very personal level, I have developed tried and tested methods of training and fighting. These methods are based on what I have found to be important through genuine experience and real violence. My goal is to help good people prepare to WIN the fight against the violent bad guy, and winning means to win physically, legally, socially, and psychologically. The elements of mindset and orientation, culture and conditioning, all play into what we need to be focusing on in training for that horrific day. I am going to lay those methods out for you here in this book.

I want to help you avoid the tragic loss that I have suffered to gain this knowledge. The fallout from violence is LIFELONG. It never stops. Failed marriages, failed jobs and careers (labeled as a felon, inability to handle the lack of respect and bad attitudes from weak, sarcastic people), an altered vision of goals, depression, problems socializing because people can't even understand the paradigm you see everything through...everything changes forever. I was raised by criminals, and lived with the worst of the worst in the house of wolves for years. I know the subject of criminal violence better than most, but, this does not define who I am. My training, my concepts and the value that I add to the world today are simply a product of it. My actions as a man define who I am. I happen to be from the place that produces your enemy, so my experience is extremely relevant to your mission. I hope you gain every advantage possible from my words so that no matter what comes against you, you can live a long and happy life with your loved ones. After all, we only get One Life.

SECTION ONE: MISSION

CHAPTER ONE: WHAT IS MY MISSION?

So, you want to save the world...

Mission defines purpose. It determines your training and gear needs. You cannot effectively train, purchase gear, or prepare in any way without first and foremost clearly defining what your overall mission is. We all have a personal "mission": what we hope to accomplish daily in our lives. We don't have to be a soldier or law enforcement (LE) to have a mission. Simply making it home (not just tonight, but every night) to live a happy life with your loved ones is a *mission*.

The very first step in any training is to identify the mission you will train for. "What is your mission?" I always ask this question first thing in the morning for every level 1 course I teach. It is amazing how often people cannot clearly answer it. If you are not clear what your mission is, you have very little guidance on how to properly equip, train and prepare. I know this sounds simple, but in the hundreds of courses that I have taught, when I ask this question most people either cannot answer or get it completely wrong.

What is a wrong answer? It is wrong when it contradicts your OWN goals. For example, someone who trains to protect themselves and their family, but intends to run head first into a fight for a stranger when neither that person or his or her family is endangered. Noble or not, if your mission is to protect yourself and make it home with your family every night, running into any random deadly situation you see is not in line with that mission. You could lose your life, and it would not have been in the defense of you or your family. Your family is left without protection.

At that point you have failed in your actual, stated mission. I would rather hear someone proclaims their mission is to fight evil wherever it appears, like Batman, than to hear them contradict their own stated mission like that. When you get into any situation where you begin to go outside of the lines of your mission, you will get into trouble. Your chances of failure increase exponentially. You are in a territory that you have not planned or prepared for. You have a higher chance of hesitation in the moment if you have a rush of clarity about engaging in a fight that may take you from your loved ones when that fight doesn't involve protecting you or them. The other actors may not be who they appear to be. Too many things can happen.

For most civilians, the mission is something like this, "To make it home, every night, with my family, for the rest of my life." At the root of it, military, law enforcement and civilians probably all have that in common, we all want to go home. What differentiates our lanes from one another are the objectives, parameters and details of the mission. So, what is your mission? To fight evil? To respond to distress signals, screams, dispatch calls? To be prepared to protect yourself and your family? Clearly identify your mission and stick to it.

Law enforcement must put the public *first,* since that is the very nature of the job to protect and serve the public. What this means is that training and gear will be guided toward this objective and this effort. That is why they throw flash grenades into rooms and not frag grenades on raids. There is a priority of life they are tasked with adhering to. They can also under certain circumstances employ force against a fleeing felon. Civilians cannot legally conduct raids or employ force against a fleeing attacker. Our rules of engagement, gear and training must be tailored to our needs according to our *mission.*

THE PERILS OF THE SHEEPDOG TRAP

What is a "sheepdog?" In its simplest form it's a buzzword used to describe anyone who is "concerned with the safety of others." It began as a descriptive metaphor for military and law enforcement, but was then, for whatever reason, spread to the civilian gun carrying community. I can see where it has *some* application in the military and law enforcement communities, if you really want to look at it that way, but I see problems in applying it to the civilian world. I do not subscribe to this mentality and I recommend that you also resist the urge to do so, as I will explain.

It is very important to clearly identify the objective of your mission. The *sheepdog* mentality will lull you into believing that it's now your job to fight crime because you carry a gun. That whole sheepdog movement is something I personally have come to detest in the training and concealed carry world. It's bullshit, especially when adopted by civilians. It implies that your mission is to protect and serve the public, at least that's how I see it interpreted all too often. The problem with this is that it often differs from what your stated mission is (to protect your loved ones and yourself), and also you do not have the legal protections that some law enforcement officer or military personnel has. Most often gun carriers lack the training necessary to effectively defend themselves within all of the boundaries, let alone having the training to defend strangers randomly.

This is just the simple truth. I spent several years working the counter in gun stores. The absolute garbage attitudes I had to tolerate that were driven completely by that mentality were insufferable. Every state has very clear self-defense criteria that must be met to claim self-defense in court. Clearly defining your mission is the first step in not violating those rules, and all too often not understanding those rules clearly is a symptom of sheepdog attitudes. That is one concern. The other concern is risking your life and freedom when it's unnecessary and not in pursuit of your actual mission. I'll tell you a story that I like to tell in classes and seminars just to see the paradigm shift happen in real-time on the audience's faces.

In one small town that I lived in, I used to stop at the convenience store and get my coffee every day for a few years. Now, when I am in the same place that frequently, I generally begin to memorize the layout and develop procedures that would cover a multitude of likely scenarios. Where are the entry and exit doors? Where is the safest backstop wall? Where are the "no shoot" areas like the cashier, front windows, etc. This is in case I am there, maybe even with my family, and something bad happens. Despite my preparedness, a fight never took place while I was there. But something much more interesting did happen. A polite young guy worked there for about half of the time I was a customer. He was always well-mannered and helpful. I recall him talking about applying for a position at the post office and waiting for his background checks and tests to come back.

Then, one day, he was no longer there. I figured he had gotten called from the post office and was on his way to a new career. Within a week, he was on the front page of the newspaper sitting on the rack at the very same store he had worked at. He had been arrested in a sting for child pornography. Apparently, they had caught him red-handed with child exploitation porn on his hard drives, making purchases, etc.

What is the point of this story? The possible price of *sheepdogging*. What if you walked into that store, and that clerk was getting robbed at gunpoint? Instead of taking the opportunity to flee and call the police thereby both helping and accomplishing your mission of making it home, you jump into your sheepdog role and engage in a gun battle with the robber. The robber shoots and kills you. What are the results? You are dead; everything you should have been is extinguished forever. Your family is now without protection, without your income and without your companionship forever. You completely failed your mission to provide for and protect them. And for what? To protect someone who was a pedophile exploiting young children in pornography.

I did not make up that story about the clerk. This is real life. The moral of the story is that you *don't know what you don't know.* Engaging in other people's fights can lead you into mistakes that you have no way of knowing you will make. Your chances of avoiding this can be greatly increased by simply clarifying your mission and sticking to that mission's objective. If you are a civilian, then be a civilian and protect yourself and your loved ones. If you are a law enforcement officer, then be a LEO.

Whatever your role is, you have a serious mission. Leave the sheepdog bullshit to the fantasy gunfighters. Real sheepdogs are dumb animals that do not prey on anything, live completely off of handouts, and their sole job is to protect even dumber animals, so they can be used and eventually slaughtered by their owner. That's your spirit animal?? They don't "protect" anyone. If you want to fight wolves, either be a wolf or go get a uniformed job and be a hunter.

I absolutely cannot express to you just how mandatory it is that you clearly define your mission. Before you go any further, sit down and write out the one sentence that defines what your real mission is. The example I like to use is this:

OBJECTIVE CHANGES WITH CIRCUMSTANCES

The reason that we differentiate objective from mission is because the objective will change according to the circumstances. If your mission is to make it home safely with you and your family each night, what happens if you are already home? What if you are out in public alone? With your family? It is much easier to stick to your mission when you understand that it isn't always achieved by fighting. Sometimes, there are different paths that you can take to achieve the same destination. Knowing that, as you begin training skills and building your mindset, will allow for a more holistic approach to your preparation.

For the civilian, your objective is probably to protect yourself and family from violent attack. If that fight comes to you someday, then winning that fight on all fronts--physical, legal, social, psychological--is your mission. Sometimes winning is done by avoiding the problem altogether. Sometimes it is accomplished by escaping. Other times, it may be unavoidable that physical confrontation takes place. The mission remains the same, but the immediate objectives will change according to the circumstances at hand. Procedures will change within objectives as well. The procedures you use for risk assessment and fighting when out in the public with your family will be dramatically different than the procedures used at home in the middle of the night. Furthermore, the parameters and rules of engagement can change in important ways as well. However, the basic objective will be the same. Identifying which objective, you should have once challenged is a critical component of accomplishing your overall mission.

OBJECTIVE # 1: AVOIDANCE

In any situation, your first objective is to avoid violent confrontation if it is at all possible. Avoidance is a guaranteed way to accomplish your mission of making it home physically, unscathed and legally whole. Violence, win or lose, is a very expensive event. It is very expensive physically, psychologically, socially and financially. The risk is always high. You can die. You can be maimed or rendered mentally incompetent. You can go to prison. It is important to make avoiding all that risk the desired option. In other words, unless violence is unavoidable, my primary objective is to avoid problems and conflict, so I can accomplish my mission with low-cost effort. This is an objective that is primarily prepared for through mindset, awareness and self-control. Having properly identified parameters and rules, which we will cover soon, will give you the guidelines needed to focus your awareness into the proper directions and to maintain the self-control to utilize the information that your awareness feeds to you.

Deterrence is another one that can fall into the avoidance category, and I will go deeper into deterrence in the "Concealment" section of the book. While it's worth noting here that both Overt Deterrence and Covert Deterrence can be effective, most people's elementary understanding of deterrence is way off base and does not work the way they think it does. Overt Deterrence tells me everything you're playing as a strong suit, which allows me to strategize against and around your strengths. Covert Deterrence tells me you are unpredictable, making it difficult for me to strategize and find certainty in my attack plans. (Later on, we'll examine how deterrence does and does not work within the predator's realm.)

Sometimes avoidance comes in the form of just being smart enough to not go around bad people in bad places. Other times, it can take on a much more complex form and you will have to make very hard decisions between two bad choices. Avoidance of violence is almost always worth it. If you can come out whole and removed from any danger, just do it. Fuck your ego. And if your girl looks down on you for backing down, chances are she will leave you when you get locked up defending her honor. Trust me, there are women out there that would prefer you home safe.

OBJECTIVE # 2: ESCAPE

When avoidance is not possible, but you have an avenue of escape or evasion that will not endanger yourself or other innocents, this becomes your primary objective. It is my strong advice that you escape or evade whenever possible rather than engage in violence. Remember, what we are seeking to do is accomplish our mission daily. Engaging in violence when you absolutely do not have to unnecessarily jeopardizes everything that you love and everything that you are attached to. In many states, it is illegal to engage in a fight when a clear avenue of safe retreat existed. Whether you agree with this or not does not change what the law says. Even in states that have *stand your ground* laws, you are taking a legal risk anytime you choose violence over an option to evade. Regardless of what the law says, it is true that unnecessary risk is, well, unnecessary. Why would you risk everything you stand to protect and love if it was avoidable? Pride and ego put more souls in the ground and behind bars than any other factors.

Learn the self-control craft of a true warrior who is loyal to his mission and does not take unnecessary risks that threaten the purpose for being here. I also group de-escalation into the escape category. If you are so close that you failed to avoid it, and too close to simply run, you are now trying to buy yourself the time or opportunity to escape. Escape doesn't have to mean running away as fast as possible; that is only one way to escape. Your ability to negotiate and de-escalate can be a real part of your escape plan. This also requires great self-control, as de-escalation is nearly impossible if your anger or ego are in the way. De-escalation, if you get the opportunity to use it, is typically the last chance you will get to avoid the violence. If de-escalation fails, and all avenues of escape are cut off, we move on to the ugly truth of objective #3.

OBJECTIVE # 3: WIN THE FIGHT

Sometimes, the fight is just unavoidable. You have no chance to practice avoidance. You are left with no avenue of escape. You must fight. Your objective is to win that fight. The rest of this book will deal heavily with preparing you for that fight. But remember, winning takes more than just winning the physical fight. To accomplish the mission today, you have to make it home with your family with everyone physically, legally and psychologically whole. This requires your training and objectives to be built around very clearly identified boundaries. Those boundaries are both internal and external. Internal boundaries are your mission parameters, what you are willing to kill or die for. External boundaries are the rules of engagement, the laws and use of force policies that govern what will happen to you *after* the fight is over. I identify 4 main categories that are needed to win a fight:

1. The physical fight. You must have the skills, orientation and conditioning to win the physical fight
2. The legal fight. You must be cleared of any criminal and civil charges.

9

3. The social fight. You must remain socially whole and not lose friends, family, jobs and careers over the aftermath.
4. The psychological fight. You must survive psychologically and not be destroyed by PTSD, fear, anger and other depreciating mental conditions that may overtake you after a life-changing event of violence.

From now on, when you are training or thinking about "winning the fight" please include these categories into your thought process and decision making. You cannot be completely prepared for a fight without considering all of them.

CHAPTER TWO: MISSION PARAMETERS

INTERNAL BOUNDARIES: ATTACHMENTS AND SELF-CONTROL

What are you willing to kill or die for? The parameters of the mission are set by your attachments in life, how far you are willing to go to protect them. In other words, you are attached to your loved ones and your own well-being. Are you willing to die for them? Again, something that seems simple actually requires a serious introspective look. You must know what you are willing to do, and what you are willing to sacrifice, to accomplish your mission. You must know the potential of what it may take to get there. Parameters are basically the boundaries of how far you are *willing* to go. This is differentiated from the boundaries put on you by outside influence, e.g. the laws. These parameters are internally created boundaries, and are directly affected by your attachments to your loved ones and to your own life. I'll give you an example of a couple of guys without clearly defined parameters:

DYING FOR A SPOT IN LINE

In 2012, a shooting took place in a Norfolk, Virginia pharmacy. A well-known surveillance video shows the gunfight develop between two men in a Rite Aid. One man was killed in the fight. The trials ended in a hung jury TWICE; they could not decide whether to convict based on what is shown in the surveillance video. Eventually, 3 years later the charges were dropped. Take a few minutes to find and watch the video on YouTube (search for "Rite Aid shooting surveillance video"). The man walking around on the cell phone is Bernell Benn, a concealed carry permit holder. Witnesses reported Benn was pacing around speaking loudly and profanely on the phone. The second man who walked up was Raymon Colorado, a former Sheriff deputy and auxiliary deputy. Benn believed Colorado got in line by cutting in front of him, which begins the encounter.

I've seen countless postings on social media asking the question, "Who was wrong?" This is a great case to ask that question about. It's not clear cut. It's muddy; the lines are blurred. You must always keep in mind that when it comes to deadly force, it will not always be cut and dry where you will *obviously* be a good guy and the other guy is *obviously* bad. It's a good reminder that if you are prepared to use deadly force to defend yourself, you better be EQUALLY prepared to articulate *why* you used that force to the law.

Benn, the man on the cell phone, was not anywhere near the counter or in any position where you would even suspect he is in line. I consider it utterly rude and arrogant to expect others to consider your mere presence in the room to be an indicator of you being in a line that is 10-12 feet away from you and your public cell phone conversation. I'm sure most of us have encountered these arrogant types out in public. If you are in line, then get in line. Period. There was no reason whatsoever that the second man, Colorado, would have any reason to believe anyone was in line in front of him when he walked directly to the next unoccupied spot in line. After the Colorado is in line for more than 15 seconds, oblivious to the situation about to develop, Benn approaches him presumably to say something like, "hey you know I'm next in line; I'm in front of you." That moment is what I will call the emotional crossroad.

What are your choices here if you are Benn? The polite thing to do would be to realize that you did not courteously stand in line like a reasonable person and therefore forfeit your spot in line. He obviously wasn't having any of that. He chose the other option of standing his ground. What are your choices here if you are Colorado? The least confrontational thing to do would be to give in and let the guy go in front of you. He, likewise, wasn't having any of that and chose to *stand his ground*. Of course, that pivotal moment did not lead immediately to a shootout. These two men were presented with several more opportunities to avoid or escape, which obviously neither of them did.

At the point where Colorado pepper sprays Benn, *there was no visible provocation of actual violence in the form of immediate oncoming violence.* You see him position the pepper spray in his hand long before he uses it, having firmly decided that *no matter what,* he is NOT giving up his spot in line. In other words, the confrontation was still in a verbal phase, no physical action had been initiated until Colorado employed pepper spray. *Colorado, based on the video, committed a clear escalation from verbal to physical without an apparent physical provocation.* Benn was hovering and no doubt being verbal, but all he was doing was talking, and still on the cell phone. Remember, it does not matter what someone is *saying.* When it comes to justifying your actions in a confrontation it only matters what they are *doing* in the moments prior to you making physical contact.

Immediately after the pepper spray was employed, Colorado pursues the temporarily blinded Benn and attempts to head him off in another aisle. When he finds him, he found more than he bargained for, and a gunfight raged in full force, which of course Colorado did not survive. From the choices made by these two men at this pivotal emotional crossroad, one of them is dead and the other is facing multiple trials. Over a spot in a line. A spot in a line that would have amounted to what? 5 minutes of their life at the most? What the fuck?

Rather than asking "Who was at fault?" or "Who was wrong?" I would like to ask a more important question: "Was a spot in line at Rite Aid worth dying over?" Let me say that again: is it worth dying, leaving your family behind and forever extinguishing anything you would go on to do with your life over one spot in a line at a store? A three to five-minute delay in your day? Hell no! It isn't worth it. Conversely, is it worth going to prison for the rest of your life over? Or in the very least consuming your entire net worth and a year or two of your life in serious legal battle? Hell no! It isn't. It's a completely bullshit reason to die or kill for, and it's childish.

Don't make the mistake of thinking that Benn came out of this ok, either. 3 years of hellish jury trials and news coverage undoubtedly took a financial, social and personal toll on his life. He clearly is not truly a winner in this situation. He's a survivor. This was a clear case where two men, who were carrying guns, had not clearly defined what their mission was nor did they have firmly established parameters in line with that mission. If you are willing to go violent over a spot in line, your parameters are either non-existent or you are mentally fucked up. This is just one example of not doing the steps I suggest in this book, and how you will pay dearly for that mistake.

YOU DO NOT CONTROL OTHER PEOPLE

Before you engage in the next stupid argument over some childish principle like a spot in line, ask yourself, "What am i willing to kill or die for?" Don't think *standing your ground* over a spot in the checkout line is a life or death decision? See the above cited case again. This is especially true if you are carrying a gun or other lethal weapon. You have the means to deliver deadly force. You may believe you are just standing your ground assertively, but you have no control over how the other person will react and escalate. Nor can you accurately predict their reaction. This recalls a hierarchy of escalation, for which I credit to Marc MacYoung:

"Nice people fall to the manipulator.
The manipulator crumbles under the assertive.
The assertive shrinks before the aggressive.
The aggressive have no plan for the assaultive.
The assaultive are unprepared for the homicidal."

How far are you willing to go, *and how do you know that the other guy will not be willing to go farther*? If you pepper spray someone (assaultive), how do you know they will not turn around and shoot you (homicidal)? You don't. And if you are willing to *offend* you better be willing to *assault*. If you are willing to *assault*, you better be willing to *kill*. If you are willing to kill, you better be 100% justified. What are you willing to kill for again? Wait, you won't kill over a spot in line, but you will assault over it? Then the other guy decides that he is willing to kill to stop your assault, and now YOU must kill or be killed. This is how violence *works*. This is exactly how it worked at Rite Aid that day in 2012. Once you open that door to violence, anything from aggressive to homicidal can come out; you don't get to choose which one and there's no putting it back in once it comes out.

Now, I understand how some of you feel. Why should we have to "cower" to bullies and arrogant, rude people? But if this is how you are thinking, then you very likely may be heading for great loss like the men in this video. Walking away from a childish argument and going on with your life is *not* cowering. There is no real lasting effect on you, other than your hurt feelings and pride. Think about that deeply. I am the first one to say that you have the absolute right to defend yourself with deadly force from violent attack. In fact, I will even train you to be good at it. But there are some qualifiers for what is and what isn't self-defense.

In short, here are some hints whether it is self-defense or not: When you have used deadly force, the attack on you must not have been created *or escalated* by you, it must have presented a reasonable belief in imminent serious bodily harm or death, and you must have not had the opportunity or ability to leave without a fight (in some states). At various times during the incident, both men in the video were out of bounds on all three of those criteria (it's no wonder a jury couldn't decide when their only choices are two idiot participants).

Self-control is the #1 mistake made in the avoidance category. Having a strong and effective mindset isn't just about always being alert and ready to jump into action. Proper mindset

15

involves enormous self-control. Not only for anger and ego issues, but for fear and other emotional spikes which will disrupt your rationality and push you into crossing the line away from self-defense and into criminal charges. You cannot kill over property, and you sure as hell cannot kill over hurt feelings. Get over it. Relax. Go on with your life. Some things just aren't worth it. And since this is such an important topic, I will give you another example. I give these examples because I have seen, and participated in, this type of senseless violence and watched the devastation afterwards. I have known countless people rotting in prison, in mental hell, because they made stupid mistakes just like these.

A STABBING IN WISCONSIN

In the spring of 2015, Wisconsin father of 5 was stabbed to death over an argument during a fishing outing in yet another horribly unfortunate event to draw some wisdom from. I am as pro-gun and pro-self-defense as it gets, but that doesn't mean that every problem is a nail just because you have a hammer.

As KARE Channel 11 Minneapolis reported: (emphasis added)

"Sheriff Peter Johnson says two groups of men, two anglers on the Minnesota side of the river and three on the Wisconsin side, began arguing around 6:30 p.m. near Interstate Park. **Over the next several hours the argument escalated**, and eventually the two men on the Minnesota side drove across the river to a boat landing where a physical altercation took place. During that fight, 34-year-old Peter Kelly of St. Croix Falls, Wis. was fatally stabbed. The three men who were involved in the fight with the victim immediately fled the scene."

So, let's look at the options available vs. the option chosen by the now deceased man:
- Call the police
- Leave the area

16

- Ignore the group

  or

- Confront the group to *correct their behavior* or teach them a lesson

Which one sounds like a *really* bad idea? The last one. Obviously, he chose the last option, confrontation, which was to become the last choice he will ever make. To me, that bares some examination since it didn't work out so well for him. Before we tear into those options, I want to remind you that we don't get to choose how someone else responds to our assertiveness. I've said this repeatedly, once you *open the door to confrontation* you have no control over which actor is going to walk out of it and, once they are out and in your face, there is little chance of putting them back in. ANYTIME you engage in a confrontation you are opening the door to ultimately lethal violence.

I know this is hard for some to understand because it is so common that most arguments just end in the verbal stage, and the few that go to blows typically end with a torn shirt and a bloody nose. Don't let that create a normalcy bias in your analysis of what threat level you could be dealing with. The truth is you do not know what threat level the person is or how far or how quickly they are ready to take it up the violence scale. This is predictably amplified when dealing with intoxicated trouble-makers

Look at it like this: if someone is acting in a way that you do not like, and you choose to confront them, while you may be willing to be assertive or aggressive, what will you do when they respond with the willingness to actually fight? Now you must be ready to fight in return to defend yourself. Quickly, they counter your fight with lethal counter attack. You argue, he shoves, you shove back, he punches, you punch back, he pulls a knife and attacks. Now someone will be mortally wounded. Will it be you? Or, will you crank your own level up to the lethal force notch to defend yourself? Is this what you set out to do when you stepped up to confront them? Were you prepared to kill or die for the cause behind your motive to confront? Or did you think you would correct their behavior? Did you think you would smack them around and teach them a lesson? So, back to our options. Sure, he could have called the cops. That could go either way. Maybe the rowdy assholes would have left, maybe not. Maybe they would have come back for revenge. Who knows? He could have chosen to ignore the group. As I understand the story, he was on the *opposite side of the river* and their antics were not initially directed at him in any way, perhaps he was just upset that his nice quiet fishing trip was being ruined by loud obnoxious people. He also could have chosen to leave the area completely. He could have packed it up, headed off to a different fishing hole, or said the heck with it and headed back home to his family.

Ignoring them for a few hours or leaving the area all together may seem hard to do, but what is hard is a family of 5 kids now living suddenly without a father for a lifetime. What do you think is harder?

If he had a do-over, what do you think he would choose?

I know, I can hear the "*stand your ground!*" arguments already, "what are we supposed to do, cower and run every time someone is obnoxious?" Or, "If we let miscreants run us off we're *letting them win!* Eventually we'll have no place to go!" While I understand this sentiment completely, I also deeply understand the true costs of real violence: Death, fatherless children, grieving spouses, and prison where criminal animals truly do control the environment you will live in 24/7. These are actual costs of violence. While you may believe you are the "good guy" and you will prevail and be cleared of all charges, the reality is you will be playing a very dangerous game with extremely high-stakes-- including all of the above--and the final physical, psychological, social and legal outcomes are unpredictable.

Since we clearly know the real stakes involved in the gamble of confrontation, and we also understand that we cannot predict to what level the other person will force the violence, what choice do

18

we make when a group of guys are being rowdy and ruining our quiet time? Is it a necessary confrontation? Truly necessary? If you choose the option that Peter Kelly chose, what do you really expect to accomplish? Tell me, whenever a man approaches a group of rowdy men and *tells that group of men what to do*, does it usually end well? You're going to drive across the river, across the State line, just to tell a bunch of loud guys to stop being loud; to shut up?

I think we see how well that worked out, and I think it was entirely predictable that it would result with an escalation. As reported by the StarTribune (April 22, 2015) Kelly is the one who crossed the river for confrontation, was it the knife-wielding teen who was acting in self-defense? Can you answer those questions? Let me be clear that I am not judging, I am simply presenting this story to you in a way that is very similar to how prosecutors will look at it. I am pointing out the stupidity of getting into fights when you don't have to.

This is where you must make that choice. You must decide how much your life, health and freedom mean to you. How important is it to tell your kids goodnight tonight, and every night? Is teaching some worthless piece of trash a lesson worth risking it all? Risking life for anything less than saving life is stupid. Period. Sure, we can hypothesize that if Peter Kelly had a gun it may have turned out different. Of course, it might have. It could also have ended the same way, or with Kelly facing an enormously expensive jury trial when an over-zealous prosecutor takes the fact that *Kelly willingly engaged in the preceding argument for hours and was the one who physically drove to the other side of the river for the confrontation* as grounds for a murder charge. Did I mention that the group was made up of teenage kids around the ages of 17 to 19? As dumb as it is to engage in violence, it happens all the time. Butchered people and dead bodies are not taken lightly by our legal system. There will be intense and often emotional scrutiny. I'm not telling you to cower. I'm asking you to weigh the risks against the possible outcomes to make good decisions.

COWERING VS. AVOIDANCE: KNOW THE DIFFERENCE

If, as the story goes, Peter Kelly was on the opposite side of the river, in a completely different State, then he was not being cornered. He initiated, continued and escalated the confrontation from across the river. Had he not done that and instead ignored them or left the area, that would have been avoidance, not cowering. On the contrary, if for no reason and with no provocation from Kelly the group of men came to his location, surrounded him and began being abusive, the situation would be different. The confrontation would be necessary and unavoidable. That was, by all accounts, not the situation that night. He was not cornered at the onset of the argument. He continued the argument for several hours while the group became angrier. He had, for several hours, ample opportunity to disengage or leave the area. Instead, 3 hours into the argument, he drove to the other side of the river for the sole purpose of confrontation. He subsequently died because of that confrontation. Did he make the best choices?

Levi Acre-Kendall was 19 years old the night he stabbed Kelly. He rejected all plea deals and opted for a jury trial. While he was found not guilty, he faced two charges. Yes, the legal system will charge you twice, essentially. First the jury decided whether to convict on intentional homicide. When they decided that didn't fit the case, they knocked it down to unintentional homicide and decided to deliberate on that charge. The jury was 11 to 1. One person saved young Levi from spending his young adulthood in prison. One person. What if that one person hadn't been picked for jury duty that day? See, it didn't come down to truth or justice, it came down to the opinion of one single person. We can assume that his family dumped a significant amount of money into his defense. One of the statements made by Kelly's brother after the "not guilty" verdict was delivered was something to the effect that with money you can hire a good attorney. The combination of a good attorney's argument and one person's opinion being swayed enough is all that saved Levi's life that day. That kid will never know how damn close he came to be trapped in a nightmare life forever. Kelly's life, of course, will never be returned. It is gone forever.

Let me make it clear that I am not shy about supporting the use of lethal force to stop an imminent deadly threat. In fact, a clear majority of my time is spent training for, and training others, to quickly and effectively use lethal force to stop a deadly threat. It's not a hobby for me. It is my livelihood and my professional mission. If you are not at fault for creating the problem, the threat is serious and imminent, and you have no alternative, then you must project a massive amount of violence into that bad person's center of mass and stop that threat. But ask yourself, could any of the deadly situations mentioned above have been avoided? Of course, they could have. All it would have taken was a clearly defined mission, with some clearly defined parameters about what you can and can't do, and the self-control to stay in those guidelines. Everyone would have went home and eventually forgot about what would have amounted to a small nuisance.

The more you actively pursue and engage in prolonged arguments and principle-driven confrontations, the less legal protection you have, and the higher the danger of being maimed or killed becomes. And even if you win, the aftermath can still be costly. Anyone who tells you a glorified story of what it will be like to drop some worthless criminal dead and how you should not give a shit about it clearly has not been touched by the life-changing damage of deadly bloodshed. Sometimes we learn the most not from the winners, but from the losers. I have personally known countless individuals sitting in prison from stories very similar to those I just talked about here. This shit is real.

Identify and define your parameters

It is much easier to control yourself if you have established boundaries to control yourself within. Those parameters of your mission are dictated by your attachments to your own life and to the well-being and companionship of your loved ones. You KNOW that engaging in violence will threaten all those attachments, so you will not do so unnecessarily. But if you are more attached to your ego, your "identity" and your pride, it will lead you into problems.

Self-control implies that there are boundaries to keep yourself within. Many people talk about self-control, but not many discuss constructing the guidelines within which to control yourself. Seriously think about this for a moment. In order to control something, there has to be a defined area you want to control it in; defined boundaries that cannot be broken. Self-control is literally defined as the ability to regulate one's emotions, thoughts, and behavior in the face of temptations and impulses. Later in the book we'll get into the decision-making factors, which attachments play a huge part in. For now, it's important to understand that in order for you to stay within the parameters of your mission you must clearly identify your internal and external boundaries. Those internal boundaries are basically what you are attached to and what you are willing do to protect it. This defines what you are not willing to do and what will threaten those attachments.

Often, *you* are the greatest threat to your own attachments that you claim to protect. In the above examples, the men who lost their lives or lived through harrowing legal battles did not clearly identify these parameters and they paid for it dearly, some with their very lives. The "mission" of making it home to the family was sacrificed for pride, ego, anger. If you believe that being a "warrior" is being ready to defend "honor" from mere words or inconveniences, then you have a thoroughly fucked up perspective of what being a warrior is all about. Being ready to fight is not all there is to it. You can be ready to fight and completely out of control, and when that happens you will fail at your mission ultimately. This is a definite characteristic of the criminal culture. Things like disrespect, personal space, perceived territory, "honor", and challenges to perceived authority are enough to kill or die for. Make no mistake, if you don't define your own parameters and then exercise self-control, you are no different than them, and you will end up in prison or the grave, or both, just like them.

It's not easy to do this, to control these urges. After doing years in prison, even 20 years later it's easy to identify these moments when one must maintain this self-control. Just one example from my own experiences happened recently in the gym, a public and somewhat "upscale" gym that I am a member at. I was in the sauna, and had just shut the large overhead light off to sit in the dim light and decompress after a workout. Nearly immediately after I switched the light off, a bigger guy comes in and switches the light on. I failed to let it go and asked, "Did you see I just turned the light off?" He replied, "What, you want me to turn it off?" I said "no" and let it go. He didn't let it go, however. A few minutes later he got out and turned the light off, and I thought, "well, maybe he wasn't that bad." Then, with a change of heart, he came back and for no good reason flipped the light back on from outside of the sauna. He wasn't even in there anymore and had no business fucking with the light. He was purposely fucking with me.

This is where big guys that have never been in a predator's world are at a serious disadvantage. The convict would quietly come out, concealing intentions while he dropped his combination lock into a sock and approached the punk while he was self-absorbed, from behind, and commence to beat him half to fucking death. But how is that at all in line with the mission of making it home and taking care of my loved ones? Let him learn his lessons on his own. It's not my job to teach him by sacrificing my freedom and risking it very easily escalating to a lethal force event. Without the mission being clearly defined, we cannot determine what we are really willing to fight for. Until those boundaries are defined, and we are truly committed to staying within them, we will not understand what self-control means.

EXTERNAL BOUNDARIES: LAWS

You may have heard the phrase, "there aren't any rules in fighting." This is a myth. UNLESS you are a criminal that operates outside of the rules of engagement (laws). If you are a civilian, law enforcement officer or soldier, you have very strict rules that you cannot break, or you will go to prison. As civilians, you cannot typically pursue someone who is fleeing. You are not allowed to use deadly force under many circumstances, most notably once the threat has ceased being a threat. Saying "I'd rather be judged by 12 than carried by 6" is--in my experienced opinion--lazy, misinformed and arrogant. I guarantee if you say it, you've never experienced it, or you are a criminal. Learn the laws of your mission, and *train in ways that give you the advantages to win and accomplish your objectives without breaking those rules.* Any good civilian defensive fight training will have a curriculum that is flush with adherence and reverence to the laws of the land you live in. It is a necessary component of the training.

In my home state of Ohio, there are 3 clearly established criteria that must be met before any use of lethal force can be considered justifiable. They are:

1. You cannot be at fault for starting or escalating the confrontation
2. You must have a reasonable belief in serious bodily harm or death at the moment force was used
3. You have a duty to retreat, if a safe avenue of retreat exists

I am certain that whatever state you are in will have very similar laws. The biggest difference will be the duty to retreat vs stand your ground. Now, there are caveats and case law that make all of this terribly muddy, even with "stand your ground" and "castle doctrine". Not to mention the fact that the average person's definition of "reasonable" is about as subjective as a favorite color.

However, any clear violation of these criteria will pretty much guarantee a conviction.

Asinine shit people say: *I'd Rather Be Judged by 12 than carried by 6*

This is one of the most ignorant comments spoken in self-defense talk. If you are repeating that statement, then you are not thinking the problem through. You are LAZY and arrogant, and there's a very real chance that you have at least a 95% chance of being wrong. Those are really fucking bad odds.

95% of criminal charges end in plea bargain conviction

Here is something that you probably don't know. In the United States, it has been estimated that roughly 95% of criminal charges end in plea bargain. According to a 2011 U.S. Department of justice commissioned report, "2011 U.S. Department of Justice commissioned report, "While there are no exact estimates of the proportion of cases that are resolved through plea bargaining, scholars estimate that about 90 to 95 percent of both federal and state court cases are resolved through this process (Devers citing Bureau of Justice Statistics, 2005; Flanagan and Maguire, 1990)."

That means that only 5 to 10% of criminal charges actually go to trial. So, while you are flapping your gums about being judged by 12, you are actually setting yourself up with about a 5% chance (or less) of actually even getting a *chance* to stay out of prison by convincing a jury of 12.

Don't forget, your author here is a living, breathing example of this. As I explained in my story at the beginning of the book, despite having basically a confession on many levels from my attacker, I was forced to take a plea bargain. It should be understandable that when I take my own first-hand experience into account, and combining that with overwhelming statistical data, I get pretty passionate about it. Nothing will shorten my fuse quicker than to hear someone defend the whole "I'll take it to trial" statement.

CHAPTER THREE: PRISON

IF YOU LOSE, PRISON IS A LIVING DEATH

A plea bargain means conviction, and conviction means prison time. Prison, is like dying, except you get to stay alive and watch what happens after you die, how everyone moves on without you, but you still get to hear all about it. It is truly a living death. Your friends will move on and forget you. Your spouse might hang in there for a while but eventually they will move on, too. You may not know the details either, you may have to just wonder. Did she meet someone else? When did it start? Was she already thinking about leaving before this? No one owes you any answers, and you will have all the time in the world to wonder about it all. It will drive you crazy.

Everyone will move on with their lives just like you were laid in the ground. You'll live out your days in captivity with predators much meaner than you, while your spouse lays down with someone else and your kids get their school clothes from some other guy. Or maybe they don't get any school clothes. Hell, maybe they get beat and you *do* hear about it. But you can't do shit about it. Nothing. *You are powerless to protect them*, and they know it, too. All the anger and determination in the world won't help you save them. This isn't hypothetical, and I'm not making this up. This is shit I watched men go through on just about a daily basis.

In addition to this, the very types of people you hate in society will become the kings and the natives of your world. They control that world. You will be on their schedule, and you will get up and start your day when they say it's time to get up with their loud behavior. There will be very little you control in your environment any more. Do you think you are tough? This is where you find out what you are really made of. The prison officials and correction officers will not differentiate you as a "good guy" from the "bad guys." You will be treated exactly like the drug dealing, murderous thug on your right and the rapist on your left. Can your mind even handle that?

People think prison is all violence and rape but, while there is a good dose of those things happening, prison is really an unending period of focused mental anguish. It's very purpose and the attitude of most of the staff are specifically designed to *break you*. Your anger issues will not serve you well at all. You will either learn to control that shit (like most tough guys do when they are faced with the ever-present possibility of raw, savage violence) or you will suffer immeasurably, and possibly be killed.

If loved ones pass away, you may not get to say goodbye to them. Your mother is about the only person that will stick with you the whole time. But if you're doing a serious stretch, she will die. If she is in another state, you absolutely will not get to go to the casket service. Or how about this scenario, a few days before the service for your mom's burial, you get into a fight defending yourself because some shitbag wanted to take something from you. Because you are in "the hole" --solitary confinement-- for a disciplinary (whether it's your fault or not), you will not be allowed to go to your mother's service. Some piece of shit can take away your one chance to say goodbye to your loved one. What if it was your wife, and she died unexpectedly in an accident? Or your child? You never get to say goodbye, and not one person gives a fuck. In fact, if you even show emotions about it, someone just might talk shit to you. Someone you can't just kill. Meanwhile, the world moves on without you.

You're already dead. Except, you're conscious the entire time.

I only had one grandmother that I knew at all, and I only really got to know her when I went to stay with her as a teenager in Nashville, TN. I became really close to her. She was truly a tough, admirable woman. When I went to prison, she allowed me to call her once a week, and each month she would send me one book of my choosing. One day I called her house and my uncle answered. I joked and said I meant to call grandma's house to which my uncle dryly replied, "You did." He then told me grandma had a heart attack and was unconscious in the hospital. Four days later they pulled the plug on her and she was gone. But that was all I ever knew. I didn't get to say goodbye, or visit her in the hospital, or attend her services. No more phone calls, no more books. And that is how that relationship ended for me. It doesn't even seem real over 20 years later, because I never got to say goodbye.

While that was pretty bad, I watched guys lose their mothers, wives, and children. Like I said, if your child is in another state and dies, you will NOT get to go to say your goodbyes if they are buried in that state. (Don't think she won't meet someone and move out of state.) This is just one aspect of prison that is horrible. But trust me, just about everything prison has to offer is a fucking nightmare. I have watched men literally break in irreversible ways. Some men become hardened like steel. Others' souls shatter into a million pieces.

THE HOUSE OF WOLVES

Prison is a place where criminals will violently control your daily environment. The guards do not run prison life. They are there to maintain a minimum of control, but they are not there to protect you. A guard is not going to put himself or herself directly into harm's way to save you. So, if a guard peeks into a cell block and sees 3 guys stabbing you, they will call for backup and wait for them to show up before they even think about breaching that door. Typically, they also know that the inmates just want to kill you and if they don't get in there until they're finished with the job, they won't put up much of a fight thereby lessening the danger to the officers. That's not a "policy" but it damn sure is on the mind of the experienced officer who wants to go home unharmed more than he gives a shit about your life. Do people get stabbed? Absolutely. It NEVER gets reported to the news, so you never hear about it. Stabbings and rapes do happen, frequently. You are on your own.

Do you think you can run with the wolves? Does it sound badass? The worst part about being with the worst of the worst is not the direct violence, it's the constant manipulation and deceit that make up 90% of transactions and communication. These are predators, con artists, and vile creatures with no moral compass. Despite what the movies say, most rapes happen due to a series of manipulative moves where the predator will cause the target to gain their trust, they will trick the target into debt with them, the violent intimidation will be turned on and sex will be either taken or offered as a way out of being killed.

I've seen young men's souls broken forever, right in front of my own eyes, over $30 worth of groceries. I've watched young men just starting out in adulthood get mentally broken to the point of being thorazine zombies. I remember a kid named Tommy who was, like me, a teenager when he was sent to the penitentiary. Unlike me, Tommy was not a violent kid. In fact, the judge who sentenced this kid to prison should rot in hell. Tommy was a goofy, suburban white kid from a decent family of gentle people. He played guitar in high school talent shows. He played video games and hung out with friends on skateboards. One day, he got talked into doing a B&E (breaking and entering) on a business. They got caught and Tommy was sentenced to a year or two in prison for his first and only criminal charge. He was 18 years old.

For some reason, Tommy was initially sent to Lancaster, which is known for brutal violence largely due to its inmate population being dominated by younger guys. It's affectionately known as "Gladiator School." Within two months of being there, Tommy was raped by another inmate. Repeatedly. After reporting his case (again they aren't there to protect you, per se) the prison granted him a transfer to a minimum-security prison, where he eventually went crazy and was placed on a steady diet of thorazine. It was too late. Tommy's life was over, at 18 years old. His soul was shattered like a glass vase, never to be put back together again.

An interesting story about Tommy, when he snapped, he actually snapped on me. He was in my cell block and attacked me in my sleep one night. I was sound asleep and was instantly thrust into an extremely violent confrontation right out of a dead sleep. His reasoning? Earlier that day, I had handed him a Playboy magazine *that he asked to see*, which made me a representative agent of the devil tempting him into sin. Fuck yes, you read that right. *He wanted to kill me for God.* Do you think you would love to live with people like that around you 24/7, even when you sleep? Have you ever fought some crazy fucker who is on a mission from God to fucking kill you? In your sleep? I have. And guess who got locked up in the hole? Both of us.

I'm fucking sleeping and I end up in the hole, because the guards don't give a shit what you have to say. They walk in, two people are fighting, two people go to the hole. If you're lucky they will investigate and maybe you get back out in 2 or 3 days. You better hope some "witnesses" like you, or you're fucked. But if you do get back out in a day or three, by then, you've lost the bed which became your "home," and you may end up in a shitty "neighborhood" (another less desirable section of the prison, where theft and violence are higher) as is likely when you are coming out of the hole.

If you are truly bluffing about the violence in your heart, your bluff will get called. Because I was raised by wolves myself, and had already committed a ton of extreme violence before landing there including having stabbed someone over 20 times to get there in the first place, I would not be an easy target. It didn't mean I didn't have to fight, but it did ensure that death would occur before anyone broke me in any way. *I knew that in my heart.* Wolves can sense when it is real, when your violence has teeth. If there are no teeth, you are in trouble. Many guys have trouble switching orientation and adjusting parameters. For example, you have to be so much more ready and willing to commit violence, and for reasons that you would not commit violence for on the streets. A taken spot in line or a threat in prison can lead to an entirely different outcome than those same

31

incidents happening in the free world. You are most likely *NOT* that type of person. You didn't grow up with it, and you will have a steep learning curve adjusting to how packs of wolves operate.

Literally everything that happens and every word that is spoken around you will have an angle. Predators are *always* playing for position, leverage and control over another person. Take a moment and think about how exhausting that is mentally, to have to be on high alert 24/7 for years on end. To have zero trust for any human interaction. If you ever get out, you will suffer from hypervigilance, PTSD and have trust issues beyond your wildest fucking nightmares.

Does all of this sound as cool as, "I'd rather be judged by 12 than carried by 6"? No? But, this IS what you are saying you would possibly rather live through than to put your energy into thinking about winning. If you take the "judged by 12" route, there's a 95% chance you're going to end up living in the world I just described to you. That is NOT winning. In my teaching, I talk about *winning*. Winning is not winning a fight and then losing your life savings, selling everything you own or losing your home to pay for a one to two-year long jury trial. WINNING is not winning a fight and then going to prison.

The "I'd rather be judged..." phrase also denotes a complete lack of thought concerning how to prepare for an event. What does it mean? It sounds a lot like it means, "*I'm not going to worry about the aftermath, nor am I going to put much thought into the subject, I'm killing them and screw the consequences.*" It's pure laziness and arrogance. It's a losing attitude. If your mission is to make it home with your family every night for the rest of your life, then you are openly stating that you are willing to just fail as long as you get to kill the other guy. Yes, it is possible that you may die or go to prison as a result of a fight. But rather than focusing on the possible loss, isn't it more advisable to focus on and train hard for the win? While the spirit of courageous self-defense is commendable, like it or not, there are more ways to lose than by taking physical damage. Your entire life can be ruined, and you'll wish you had died. This isn't about cowering; it's about making sure you have at least thought about how to do things correctly to have the best possible chance to maintain your legal shroud of self-defense.

If you are an instructor and teaching students this phrase, just stop it. You are fucked up. It's arrogant, misinformed, lazy and a complete violation of the trust given to you as an instructor. If you are a student and someone says that in a class, run away from that as quickly as possible. Some people, or dare I say most people, are completely clueless as to how the legal system truly functions. Some believe it will just be clear cut that they are the "good guy" and won't be charged, or that the NRA will step in and save you (as if they really take a personal interest in every single civilian in self-defense case across the country). CCW Insurance may or may not help, but it is not a savior and cannot change how the legal system operates. That insurance will not change the fact that 95% of charges end in plea bargain convictions. Once a prosecutor gets you in the crosshairs, you better have ample supplies of cash and you better have crossed all of your t's and dotted all of your i's before, during and after the deadly fight you are now charged for. Right or wrong, win or lose, it's going to be a long, expensive ride. And remember, insurance or not, the conviction rate is 95%.

Preparation, not laziness

Rather than focusing on the fact that a self-defense fight encompasses much more than just fighting or shooting, when you repeat the "I'd rather be judged..." phrase you set yourself (or the student) up with a narrow view of a gigantic problem. Self-defense involving lethal force is a multi-faceted event. But it does not need to be complex in the decision-making process if you know the clearly defined parameters and rules of engagement.

This can be accomplished with **a properly informed person operating with a controlled mindset that is completely focused on a clearly defined mission**. Rather than wasting any time or brain-power on processing the whole "I'd rather be judged..." philosophy, I suggest that it will be time better spent to begin to form the mindset around understanding the external boundaries (laws of lethal force), the internal boundaries (what I am willing to fight and die for), the fundamentals of fighting, and having a complete Clarity of Mission. Understanding this, it should become crystal clear that you need a predetermined set of information firmly planted in your head before you can process any new information correctly. In other words, you cannot control yourself if you do not have predetermined guidelines and boundaries. This goes right back to our Clarity of Mission, or understanding and staying focused on what your real mission is no matter what happens.

To put it plainly, when attacked, what is your mission? Your mission is first defined largely by the priority of life. For the average armed civilian that priority of life would be: 1. Family/Self, 2. Innocents in Public, 3. Bad Guy. Once the priority of life is established and understood, the boundaries of action are then considered. Our society's laws will dictate those legal boundaries.

For example, in my home State, you are permitted to stop a threat with lethal force if the threat is imminent, reasonably believed to be delivering serious harm or death at that moment, and you have no avenue of safe escape (to summarize). You cannot continue to deliver deadly force once a threat has ceased the attack. That is a clear legal boundary. You also are in a very bad legal position if you have to deliver lethal force in a situation that you started or escalated. Every internal and external boundary can be identified in this way, so it really is not that complex. Your mission is to keep yourself and loved ones out of harm's way. Within that, the laws determine that you are not permitted to harm the public, nor are you permitted to continue to do lethal damage to the bad guy once that attack has stopped. Here's how it comes together.

If your mission is to keep yourself and your loved ones safe, the laws dictate that you are not allowed to harm innocents and you must stop the use of force when the attack stops, then you know what you must do. IF you are attacked and you continue to punish, injure or *finish off* the bad guy, then you have abandoned your original mission of safety and you will fail. You have to clearly define what your mission is and stick to it. You have to be able to control your emotions, your fear, and your anger, or you will leave the boundaries of that mission and make terrible mistakes. So, you see, it makes a huge difference if you really identify and define these priorities, as opposed to being lazy and dumb and skipping all of that effort to just say, "I'd rather be judged…"

It's simple really. Proper mindset isn't just about being ready to fight; it's about maintaining control over yourself under pressure. Simply put, the most effective combat mindset is having extreme self-control in any conditions. You cannot control yourself if you do not clearly understand what your mission is and what the boundaries of that mission are. Those are your guidelines of control. Sometimes, that involves keeping your emotions in check. **Loosely flapping your lips about not caring about the consequences of lethal force is a serious indicator that you have little practical experience with the subject and have given little thought or practice to actually winning a confrontation.** If you disagree with me. I don't care, do what you want to. I focus on the totality of winning. Shrugging it all off with a "I'll roll the dice and see what happens" attitude is not how you get there, and that certainly is not a part of any professional instructor's training. If some day you find out truly how costly being "judged by 12" is--whether you win or lose--you'll regret ever having said that incredibly short-sighted phrase to another human being.

Don't Destroy your case for Self Defense on Social Media

As the last installment in the External Boundaries section of this book, I'm going to cover this topic because I think some of you just do not have any idea about this. If you do, and you don't care, then fine: carry on like I didn't say a word. But, if you have *not* thought about what you are about to read--in the context in which I will put it--then hopefully you will adjust your behavior a little bit to help keep yourselves out of trouble. By now, you should have a clear idea of how important it is to clearly know the laws under which you will be scrutinized after a fight.

A very important part of staying within those critical guidelines is to not run your mouth. Every day I see people posting on social media about "self-defense": memes with pictures of guns, catchy sayings and cool clichés like "Wrong House Motherfucker!" over a picture of a muzzle, and comments on posts about robberies or criminals, etc. Too often it goes like this, "that's why I stay locked and loaded! That criminal would not have lived if that was my house!" or "That's why I carry! I'll kill anyone who tries that shit on me or my family" or "He should have killed him and made sure he was dead!" Of course, there's a thousand variations of this theme, but basically the gist of it is that *you have* **predetermined that you will kill** *someone at any time, if they attack you or invade your home and you are on permanent record stating that.*

Every time you post something that even resembles this sentiment, you are weakening your case for self-defense should you ever find yourself in a violent confrontation. Every post you put on Facebook, every little comment you make on any random post from your favorite gun page or Facebook friend...all of it goes into recorded history to live forever somewhere. (Maybe it actually does last for many years, maybe it doesn't. You can't be sure, and the possibility that it does is pretty high.) In the real world, self-defense is a LEGAL term. It is a legal defense against criminal charges for the use of force in resisting an attack on the person, and especially for killing an assailant. If you are ever faced with a violent confrontation and you prevail in stopping the attack by using lethal force, you will have to articulate why you had to use the level of force that you used. You may have to say something like, "*I was FORCED to use that much force because he would have seriously hurt or killed me, and I had no avenue of escape.*"

36

Let's say that the prosecutor then goes and finds a comment you made, on a PUBLIC post someone else posted, where you articulated a serious hatred for robbers and let it be known in no uncertain terms that you will kill the first robber that tries it on you. As much as you may think that it is OK to kill a violent, horrible person that contributes nothing but pain and misery to society, as soon as you commit that thought to the cyber record you are setting yourself up for a legal nightmare. Why? By your own words, you are stating clearly that your *intent* is to kill, and it is never legal to kill anyone *intentionally*. No matter what they have done.

It is never legal to "shoot to kill". Period. I know, I know, it's not smart to shoot to wound. That's correct. So, we don't do that either. What you *do* is shoot to *stop the threat*. That is it; and that is all. If they die because of their wounds, *that was not your intent*. Your intent was to stop their violent attack, which you did not provoke in any way, when you had a reasonable and honest belief that serious bodily harm or death would result from their attack, and you had no duty to retreat.

This is obviously what you will be desperately trying to convey in court, while exposing your fear and hardship as the victim in the attack. That is going to be hard to convince the court of once the prosecutor introduces a statement you made on Facebook on February 23, 2013 in which you stated the following, *"If you come into my home uninvited, you DIE. No questions asked, I'll call 911 to pick up your body!"* (An actual quote I snagged from social media.) Hard to portray yourself as an innocent victim with that looming in the court's awareness. It's just as dangerous to say it in public.

Let's say you go into work and they are talking about a recent robbery that happened in a nearby parking lot. You openly and enthusiastically share how you have your ccw permit and you won't hesitate to *"shoot the dirty bastard's face off and leave him dead in the parking lot"* if he tries to rob you or attacks you. You emphasize how you won't hesitate to kill him. You don't give a shit, he's a "bad guy" and he's dead. Fast forward to two days later, you get mugged at knife point in a parking lot and you shoot and kill him. This is OK, right? I mean, the attacker pulled a knife, didn't respond to verbal commands, and you committed a pretty clean shoot. Well, by some magic of the universe the nice little old lady at work has come into contact with the county prosecutor, and she's telling him how she can't believe it that *"he was just saying two days ago how he would certainly kill the first person who tried to rob him."* Now what?

I'll tell you now, you're going to have one hell of an expensive and emotionally taxing legal fight on your hands. It will drain your resources, drain you emotionally, put the public on notice that you have, stress your home life and relationships, etc. All because you had to brag about killing people, which you have never done and have no business talking about in the first place. Do you think that some other factor won't come into play? Overzealous prosecutors, anti-ccw court officials, or worse--and very likely today--you become a media sensation for killing a *poor kid who only had a knife and possibly never really intended to use it, your vigilante, bloodthirsty racist, hater of the poor, can't-wait-to-kill-a-criminal, judge-jury-and-executioner gun owner*, you killed him in cold blood.

Think I'm being outlandish? If so, you haven't watched the news for the past 6 years. Most of you who speak so loosely about "killing" someone have never experienced serious deadly confrontations and have never been covered in someone's blood as they lay dying in front of you. Basically, a majority of you have no idea what you are talking about, and to people who have done it, you sound like an asshole. Learn that you don't know what you don't know.

Every state has very strict laws about the use of deadly force. These laws are the external boundaries of your mission. You can break these laws with action, or with words about your actions that show "intent". So, think about this the next time you are so inclined to post all over the permanent cyber record about your penchant for killing people. Winning does not mean winning a fight and then losing your house, your spouse, your kids, your freedom and your identity to be locked in a cage like an animal for 20 to life (where ironically you will have to defend your dignity and your life perpetually until the end of your days). Winning means going home to your family in one piece, and repeating that each day with no unnatural interruptions.

The passage of time is no safeguard, either. It doesn't matter how long ago you said (or did) something wrong involving violence. Here's a fun little story from my own past: Remember the case that sent me to prison? Before the hearings took place, there was a pre-sentencing investigation (PSI) conducted by the prosecutor to build the case against me. When I was interviewed for my PSI, the prosecutor brought up some hearsay from 15 years before.

Fifteen years before the current case ever happened! I was in fucking grade school! A dozen or more years before, I was in school with a kid named Charlie. Apparently, at the time of my case Charlie was also now as an "adult" teen and in some trouble; the pre-sentencing investigator conducting my face-to-face interview was also Charlie's probation officer. Now, mind you, Charlie had absolutely nothing to do with my case whatsoever. However, apparently, he did blame me for all of his problems in life because, according to him, I was mean to him in grade school. He was legitimately telling his probation officer that he was fucked up because I was mean. (The truth was that he was an instigating little shithead in school, but that's beside the point.)

I will never forget how the officer just kept repeating, "You shouldn't have picked on Charlie" over and over, as he closed my PSI folder and ended the interview. The look on his face told me exactly what he was thinking, and I am 100% convinced Charlie was a huge influence in that conclusion. Of course, we know what he recommended, and I was convicted and sentenced to prison.

Being able to defend yourself with clear justification for your actions and decisions is just as important as being able to defend yourself with fists or a gun. There's more than one way to lose, and lose is exactly what you will do if you run your mouth or establish a mean or violent reputation. Quit setting yourself up for failure. Be a positive example for the right to self-defense. Articulate your reasons well. Do not discuss deadly violence loosely. One day your life may depend on everything you have ever said about the subject, and every way you have prepared, and every class you have taken. Everything you do or say is a permanent record that can be used against you at any time in the future, no matter how long it has been. Make sure you have a clearly defined mission with very clear internal and external boundaries. The Rule of Law does not automatically know you are a good guy. Stop assuming you are protected, because you are not. You are the only one who controls your actions and words. This is of extreme importance because, someday, others will judge you harshly by those actions and words.

One final note on *talking "tough"*

I try to stay fairly positive in the public and on social media. I mainly just ignore the negative shit everyone is always so caught up in, the stuff that makes people hate each other and want to fight in the streets. However, I see this society going in a direction that I am positive it does not know it is doing. It's not where it "thinks" it is going. All this talk of violence, mass violence, political violence, of killing...some of us have lived in that dark world where beasts eat the innocent, and even bigger beasts eat those beasts. That spirit has been long self-contained in the shadows, the drug world, the prisons, the ghettos and the third world countries where most of you only catch a glimpse of it. The snarling spirit of *pure violence*. Not your high school or bar brawls, but the kind of violence that makes human beings systematically dismantle each other, mutilate one another, murder families and leave women and children crying, and dead, in the streets. I recognize glimpses of this familiar beast out in the open today, mowing people down in the streets, frothing at the mouth and gnashing its teeth in the faces of once normal people.

Be careful what you wish for. Those of you who are calling for the violence, and working hard to make it happen are clearly not the ones who know that spirit well. The ones who have that pure violence in their hearts are waiting in those shadows for you to open that door. So be very careful *soft ones*, because when the real wolves are running free in the streets you'll find out just how afraid of the dark you really are.

Have a wonderful day. Hug your loved ones and do something nice for someone today.

Self-Defense may not be what you think it is

Self-defense is not a fighting style. When someone says, "I'm taking self-defense classes" they are almost always talking about some form of martial art training. However, very rarely will any of those classes or courses teach anyone about the rules of engagement or when you can or can't use the skills they are teaching to harm another person. I would argue that it is not self-defense education if the laws and rules are not front and center in the very design of the style, skills, techniques and instruction. Is post-event articulation to establish justification woven into every single move, task and scenario? If the answer is no, then you are not taking "self-defense" classes.

I know this is nitpicking on semantics, but this is an important distinction. Self-defense is a *legal term*. "Self-defense" is what you say when the police show up after you have defended yourself. It is the phrase you utter when standing in a courtroom because of a lethal force event. Self-defense is NOT jiu jitsu, boxing, krav maga, kali knife fighting or any other fighting style or training method. For us to truly respect the laws, it is important to understand that self-defense is the term that is exclusively defined strictly by those laws for the purpose of us being able to defend ourselves legally, especially for using deadly force. Since it has such a very critical meaning, I strongly suggest that we use it properly in our training and fighting lexicon.

The problem that I see caused by the loose application of the term "self-defense" is that the real meaning of it is ignored. By this I am pointing out the fact that a great majority of people who are training in (and those who are teaching) a martial art or weapon system will almost always have two characteristics: they call their craft "self-defense training", but they cannot articulate what the laws covering the use of force are in their state. Not only is this a misuse of the term "self-defense," but it does absolutely nothing to promote a more complete education about self-defense that will include the critical element of the laws. Therefore, I emphasize the importance of knowing and understanding the rules of engagement that you live under as part of your Clarity of Mission. It is completely YOUR responsibility to learn and understand the laws of your state, as well as any state that you may be visiting or working in. Any training that is pursued should be absolutely built around the adherence to those laws: every drill, every technique, every philosophy. This is self-defense education and training. Take it from someone who was quick to violence and slow on legal knowledge. I lost more than I can ever get back because of it.

CHAPTER FOUR: RISK ASSESSMENT

Risk Assessment can also be referred to as threat response assessment. However, I prefer risk assessment because it encompasses more than just assessing an active threat. Risk can be defined as all the variables you will have to consider in a developing situation. What is the risk level, what are the parameters and laws I face, what is the risk to myself and others if I proceed with avoidance? If I proceed with escape? If I proceed with fighting? Remember our three main objectives. Risk assessment is where the decision is made on which of those to choose. This can change throughout a situation as the degree of danger raises or lowers. In other words, the objective of escape is abandoned once one is about to be cornered and inevitably will have to fight. Risk assessment is specific to a situation, and must be developed with your mission in mind. Therefore, it is included in the Mission chapter. For example, the risk assessment model of you walking into a store to buy your coffee would be vastly different than a law enforcement officer walking into the same store responding to a violent person call. Assessing risk at home is much different than in public. You do not set up a perimeter with strict rules against invasion when you are out in the public, but this is what you do at home.

Situational awareness is closely related to risk assessment. After all, without situational awareness assessment will happen too late, if at all. Developing a solid risk assessment model will naturally improve your situational awareness. It raises the importance of catching early cues and warning signs, which in turn causes you to pay attention more. The result is that you develop a solid risk assessment model that helps you make appropriate decisions while systematically developing your situational awareness to a higher level. This is accomplished through training, lecture/research and then application and practice.

Risk assessment is just that, you are seeing your options between objectives (avoid, escape, fight) and weighing the risk of each option against the level of threat you may be facing. It begins well before any danger signs come up. Your awareness level is focused on your environment in a relaxed but actively scanning manner. It is like running a virus scan on your computer in the background. You can still focus on what you are doing--eating, enjoying time with family, working--but you will be immediately alerted if something begins to be *abnormal* in your environment. This is accomplished by taking what we know about our mission, our boundaries, our objectives and our environment and then processing it through situational awareness and abnormality cues.

SITUATIONAL AWARENESS

Situational awareness is a phrase that gets thrown around in the training world, but few ever explain what it really means. In its simplest form it means being aware of your surroundings, of the situation you are currently in. But in a training context, we need to expand upon that and make it a trainable, repeatable skill that we progressively become better at. Now that we understand clearly what our mission is, how far we are willing to go to accomplish it, and what the legal boundaries that we must work within are, we can build a mindset of preparedness around this information.

DEVELOPING *WIDE-BAND* SITUATIONAL AWARENESS

There are a lot of cliché statements repeated over and over ad nauseum in the training world. Many of those statements refer to situational awareness, the most popular being, "Keep your head on a swivel!" While it is true that it depends on how you interpret it, honestly, I think that any shallow interpretation is going

44

to miss the essence of what situational awareness is and how it actually works. If we think what happens when we begin to detect a threat, we see that the main thing that changes is that *our focus actually narrows with each increase in intensity.* This is critically important to understand. The tenser and focused you are, the smaller your field of awareness actually becomes. As the threat becomes more apparent, you become more fixated on that particular threat.

I'd like to point out the most common mistake I see in the gun carrying community: mistaking high intensity for wide-band SA. Picture the most ridiculous culprit, he's wearing tactical pants, tactical boots, requisite shirt to hide obvious gun gear, and his eyebrows are pulled into the center with a purposefully intense look on his face as his head is literally on a swivel, attempting to look in all directions at once.

While this is an extreme example, I think most of us have met this guy. Especially if you've worked in gun stores or gun shows! Either way, it's indicative of taking the SA concept in the wrong direction. It's like looking and listening through a tube, as opposed to looking and listening without constraints. Imagine if you taped a large cardboard tube over your eyes and you could only see through it. Then walk into a public place. You would literally have to turn your head in every direction to see anything and would experience a total loss of peripheral vision. Having too much SA intensity can have a similar effect on your ability to see and hear things. As we can see with the conditions of awareness, your focus intensifies onto a specific focal point. The counterpoint to this is that your broader awareness diminishes.

That is why stories about people involved in lethal force events have no recollection of outside factors like how many rounds were fired, who was around at the time, if someone other than the threat said or did something, and so on. This happens because under the threat of death or imminent serious harm our focus of awareness becomes so amazingly intense we experience auditory and visual exclusion. Our brain simply blocks out everything it does not deem vital to surviving the threat directly in front of you. I can personally vouch for this. I have experienced all levels of this up to and including auditory and visual exclusion. I can even remember specifically having tunnel vision for several minutes *after* the engagement, where I clearly did not see what was going on outside of the direction I was looking in even without a specific threat to focus on anymore. I can also vouch for this happening less with subsequent events as I grew more accustomed to operating at that elevated level. You may not have the opportunity to spend years on end in hostile environments so that you can develop this immunity, so you must cultivate a wide-band SA through training and conditioning.

Being in a relaxed-ready condition will give you the widest-band of situational awareness radar possible. It is above the oblivious and not paying attention condition, but below the point where awareness focus begins to narrow. It is the sweet spot. This allows you to see a wider field and hear more of what is going on, specifically giving you the ability to hear in directions that you are not looking in. This is what will allow you to relax and enjoy your life, while you run a constant background scan for *abnormalities* in your environment.

ABNORMALITIES

Your daily environments are pretty "normal" most of the time. What I mean by this is we usually spend our time in environments that we have been in before and have become accustomed to in the way things *should* be while we are there. Because most public or social environments have a normal range of sounds and activities, we can pick up abnormalities in that environment very easily. It is also true that dangerous things have often have very recognizable sounds: gunshots, screams, screeching tires, and even just raised voices sounding angry, to give a few examples. So, abnormalities are immediately recognizable because they are both out of place and they can be threatening in and of themselves. While both do not have to be true at the same time, you will typically get one cue or the other if you are paying attention.

Imagine you are walking down the sidewalk, very close to the street. You are enjoying your walk, maybe talking with a companion, and are surrounded by the normal sounds of the street: cars driving by, people talking, maybe even horns blowing. You are relaxed, but generally aware in your widest available band of SA. A quiet scan is running in the background listening and watching for abnormalities. Unless you hear or see one, there is no reason to become excited or to begin to narrow your awareness. You need to keep it as open as possible. Suddenly, somewhere behind you a tire loudly screeches across the pavement. Immediately you narrow your focus and access the risk, "What is happening and how can this affect me?" "Is this danger coming toward me?" "Do I need to take immediate action to avoid, escape or fight?" The screeching tires were a highly recognizable abnormality in the environment. It required your immediate attention. You cannot be looking in all directions at all times, so you must begin to cultivate a system of environmental cues both visible and audible, that you can rely on to activate your risk assessment as quickly as possible. (We should be, by now in this book, beginning to understand how the different components of preparedness all work together. Understanding Mission, parameters, objectives, conditions of awareness, risk assessment...all of this comes into play when the moment arises. (Any skipped or underdeveloped component will lower the effectiveness of your actions overall.)

Cues do not have to be immediately recognizable either. Abnormalities can be non-definite in nature. One example of this is sketchy behavior by strange individuals: You are walking down the street with your partner, at night, on the edge of downtown. People are milling about here and there, walking to their next bar stop or making their way back to their cars. In this environment people are moving or huddling with a purpose, typically. As you are walking, you notice two individuals, one on each side of the sidewalk that look out of place based on their behavior and positioning. They appear to be together, but are not being social. They have hoods pulled up over their heads. They are positioned diagonally in what *could* be a superior ambush position. They have their hands in their pockets. How many abnormalities can you count there? Take any one of those behaviors alone and it doesn't seem very alarming. But, as things begin to stack up, our level of alarm goes up. Eventually, your brain will just automatically assess matches for cues and once it picks up on a minimum amount of matches your alarm bells will go off. This will cause your risk assessment to kick into high-gear and your SA will become more focused. (But remember, don't allow your band-width to narrow to the point that you shut out the rest of your environment!)

At this point, Objective #1 avoidance will be your goal. You cross the street and walk on the other sidewalk. Now, you notice they also begin walking in that direction as well. Your focus narrows even more, but not too much! You are still swimming in open water, so to speak! Stay aware of what's in front of you, any alleys or doorways, etc. They cross the street and now are directly following 25 yards behind you. Objective #2 escape is now a goal. You're not running yet, but you do not want to let them close the gap on you.

You can imagine any type of ending to this scenario. The point should be driven home now that abnormalities in your environment can be your main cues for danger or possible danger and they are most observable from a relaxed state of awareness. Risk assessment will guide you through your risk assessment model and conditions of situational awareness, which will hopefully guide you through to mission success at the end of the day. Being able to be in a relaxed state and enjoy your family, friends, and life, yet still be aware enough to deal with serious problems as they arise, is the goal. Developing a system of cues based on abnormalities is a great place to start cultivating that awareness.

DETERRENT BEHAVIOR DO'S AND DON'TS

We've all heard the phrase, "Look like a hard target!" That is not really the best advice. Again, with the clichés, there are a ton of them in this category. "Look hard at anyone you suspect." "Stand up tall, push your chest out, posture with authority and make eye contact." The list goes on. While all of this may sound like good advice to not appear as a weak and easy target, the mistake is made by assuming that trouble only comes from bad guys looking for a weak and easy target! (This will be covered in more detail later in the Target Analysis vs. Target Selection section of this book.) It's simply not true.

In fact, posturing this way can even incite the violence. If you behaved in some of these ways in prison, puffing your chest and making authoritative eye contact, you very well may get the chance to back that up. No. You WILL get the chance to back that up, IF you see it coming. They might just decide to teach you a lesson about ambush tactics. Even within the trained and *refined* version of myself today, I can feel the convict rise up inside when some random guy makes authoritative eye contact or postures toward me. There are times when making eye contact at the wrong time will be an invitation.

There is an art to appearing confident and capable without appearing challenging. While there is way too much depth in that topic to delve all the way to the bottom in this book, suffice it to say that you need to put thought into how you will appear. One of the best exercises I have ever heard on how to get a perspective of this is to become the bad guy. What?? No, I don't mean *become* the bad guy. I mean think *like* him and choose victims based upon appearance. (I do not know where I first heard this so please forgive the lack of a citation or credit here.)

The next time you are out in public, do this exercise by looking around and picking who you would and who you would not rob or attack. Categorize them and list the reasons why you would avoid certain people. Next, take that list of deterrents and begin thinking about how you can emulate that behavior to make yourself seem less of a target. You will find reasons that are outside of the obvious cues that you are thinking about now.

While this is a great exercise at the basic level, it doesn't deal with the intricacies of the wide ranging personalities and motivations that bad guys have. However, it will work for the average predator who is looking for an easy source for a resource. The one who wants something you have (a resource) will be looking for the easiest way to get it, and that typically does not involve fighting. So, they will pick the easiest appearing targets. For the real violent predator, a different technique is needed. In the prison combat culture, we developed a *feel* for this. *What was the right amount of strength balanced with not issuing a challenge for no reason*? It usually had more to do with concealing abilities and appearing unpredictable than it did with appearing to be a badass. The bad guy you face could very likely be a convict himself, or simply a product of the criminal combat culture in general. So, he will see things very similar to how I am describing it here. I have had close calls out in public when I did not control my eyes well enough and locked too long with another predator. I can remember at least once where the guy escalated to the point of walking into me with the "shoulder bump" in the mall. Which I ignored, with some effort.

The violent predator doesn't necessarily want a resource, but wants to use you for some fantasy or personal end. That could be, from my own interpretation, anything from beating your ass just for the sake of dominant violence, all the way to kidnap and rape. The one you should be training for is the extremely violent and experienced fighter. Prepare for him, and you will have prepared for all of them. Walking around all jacked up with super-tight shirts and tactical pants and your pockets lined with the visible utility clips of knives, lights, multi-tools and whatever tactical badassery you found with a clip on it is not going to deter a truly violent individual. Honestly, the ones it will deter would be deterred by your presence and confidence minus all of the bullshit show props. If you are a smaller person, a female or have some

50

visible limitation, don't feel defeated. Your confidence will take you far. A properly concealed weapon you are trained with will take you even farther if it gets bad.

Because you do not know what kind of bad guy you are drawing, my best general advice is to make eye contact enough to say, "I see you" but no longer. Your eyes can convey or betray your true emotions. Be careful with the message you send. In fact, do not look at people without consciously knowing what message you are speaking with your eyes, period. This is a good policy in all communications. Beyond that, you will need to trust your intuition and feel the situation out to determine if you need to avoid, escape or fight (even just on an eye contact level). There truly is an art behind silent communication, and it takes years to develop it as a predator or in a predator's world. Begin working on that now.

STOP LOOKING *FOR* THINGS AND START LOOKING *AT* THINGS

I run a drill on my range, typically in higher courses, where I set up a target scenario behind some barrels and have students work their way through a series of shoot/no-shoots to get to "clearing the corner." Almost inevitably all students fail the first run, even after we talked all day about looking at things and not for things, etc. They forget all of it. They come around the corner and lose decision making ability, or they start blasting at the first black t-shirt (designated bad guy) that they see, neglecting to see the scared women and children *behind* the threat. This is based on a store robbery scenario captured on video and published on YouTube where the bad guy was able to control hostages through sheer fear and could turn his back on them. This is common. It is a problem that is easily solved by negotiating the corner properly and getting clear center mass hits before he has a full visual on you, and past the line of danger for the hostages in the back.

Almost every time, students run around the corner and perform either two ways: The first way is the majority response. They will lock up and completely hesitate in the line of fire while they try to process what they are seeing. They penetrate too deep for the angle of fire and now they do not have a shot, but they are exposed completely. They would be dead. The second, less used option is to burn around the corner and start blasting, clearly without making a full assessment of their situation and subsequently shooting the hostages as well.

Of course, in training these scenarios are artificial and "gamed" to certain extent, but these are very real considerations. It's always a paradigm shifting drill that I save for the end of the day to test retention and practice of what we covered. Of course, 7 or 8 hours is not enough to master being able to navigate such a decision process successfully. However, it is important to create a powerful learning moment to both show limitations, so no one leaves with false confidence, and to also demonstrate in an unforgettable way that these concepts work.

The main point of all of it is to look at things and process what you are seeing. In debriefing, almost all of the students talk about how their expectations of what was around the corner were shattered and they had a hard time regaining direction and purpose. This is because they came around the corner looking *for* something that they *expected* to see. They had a plan. *Training* is notorious for creating "plans" and plans do not work as well when they involve other humans who are not in on the plan. Procedures, however, do work. This is why we learn skills, develop techniques, and then learn to combine them into procedures to deal with a problem. There is a procedure for dealing with a blind corner as a solo actor. If you follow the steps, you will be able to observe, assess and orient as information comes in. If you go rushing in with a predetermined set of actions for an anticipated problem, you will be fucked from word "GO" when that anticipated problem doesn't materialize and something totally different unfolds in front of you. Look *at* things, not *for* things.

Situational Awareness in a Nutshell

Be smart. Relax. Remain generally alert and catalogue what and who is in your presence before you focus on whatever you are doing there. Set your awareness on the widest band possible. Develop a system of early warning cues based on acute hearing and vision, constantly scanning for abnormalities. Don't look like a scared victim, but don't go overboard and challenge everything that moves around you. Just be confident and relaxed. Need more confidence? Read this book. Get training. Build your conditioning. Test your skills repeatedly. That'll do the trick.

SECTION TWO: TRAINING

CHAPTER FIVE: FUNDAMENTALS OF TRAINING

The "cool" stuff. The part everyone wants to get to, right away. Now that we have defined mission clearly, an idea of what gear we will most likely need, and a framework for our mindset (parameters and self-control), we can design a training program that will begin to add the advantages we need to win in that mission. For the civilian, the mission is to protect self and loved ones, and in the process, stay out of the cemetery, hospital and prison. The first realization about training program design is that each action that you learn--every single drill you run--must consider and adhere to those objectives and boundaries.

Once we have clearly defined and understand what we are likely, willing, and allowed to do in a fight, we can begin to build the skills, techniques and procedures that will give us the advantages to be victorious in that fight (and within those boundaries). In the beginning, we must first be honest about our skill level and begin our conditioning there. Too many want to jump into "advanced" or "tactical" courses, when they can't even effectively define those words, let alone accomplish a complex task like safely running a gun, around other people, while moving quickly or transitioning positions, etc.

Once your mission is clearly identified, all your rules, parameters and likely demands are clearly defined, and you understand what training is and what it is not, the training program should proceed as follows:

- Skills
- Techniques
- Procedures
- Tactics
- Standards

The "Why"

It is absolutely mandatory that you fully understand the "why" behind everything you learn or perform in training. If as an instructor you cannot articulate the detailed reasons why you are teaching something, you quite simply should not be teaching it. "Because that's how it's done" or "It's the best way, trust me" are not sufficient answers. Fortunately, it became a trend in the training industry to point out this fact and social media shame anyone who couldn't back up their claims about a skill or technique being the "best" way to do something. Unfortunately, it became cliché'. It somehow remained shallow, focusing just on someone's "why", and then comparing their "why" to someone else's, and so forth. What I'd like to do here is invite you to go just a bit deeper and look for the principles behind the "why". In other words, the "why" will be based on principles that the performance needs to adhere to. For example:

Why do you teach to stagger your feet in your stance or landing position? **The "why":** to manage recoil, impacts, and be able to move.

The elements and principles behind the "why": Strength, mobility, stability, time, efficiency. In order to maintain maximum effectiveness and efficiency, we must be in a position to have as close to 360-degree impact stability and 360-degree rapid mobility as possible. Less time invested repositioning the feet means less time out of the fight.

The Greater Principles: efficiency minus time on task = effectiveness and speed are elements, and placing ourselves in positions to be in better control of those elements means we are adhering to fundamental principles of control and adaptability.

It's easy to come up with a "why", but it is nothing less than true understanding that identifies the principles behind your reasons. In all tasks, we are always attempting to adhere to principles. The problem with this, especially with the internet, is that anybody can justify their own "why." They might even be able to make it sound official and professional. That is the reason we have to dig down deeper than the "why" and examine the actual principles we are working to adhere to.

THE PRINCIPLES OF FIGHTING

John "Chappy" Chapman often says that gunfights are won in millimeters and milliseconds. He presents the primary elements of gun fighting as follows:

- Everything you do must be efficient and not waste movement
- Everything you do must minimize your time out of the fight

These can be considered phenomenal foundation elements upon which all of your "why's" will be based upon. *In other words, in every explanation of a skill, technique or procedure you should be able to explain it all the way down to why it is efficient and how it minimizes your time out of the fight.* Every single task that you train for the fight should adhere to these two principles. This is very, very important. Literally every skill and technique must adhere to these two principles if you want your training to produce high-quality results that you can depend on to protect your life and the lives of others.

My own elements of the physical part of fight training are as follows:

- Efficiency: Everything you do should be efficient. No wasted movements.
- Time: Everything you do should maximize your time in and out of the fight. Efficiency creates speed, and speed gives you time advantage.
- Strength: Everything you do should begin and end in a position of strength. You cannot attack effectively (in most cases) from a physical position of weakness. You cannot

defend effectively from a physical position of weakness. Therefore, I emphasize in all of my training that all movements and weapon manipulations happen inside of the "strength triangle", where elbows are locked to ribs and hands are in a strong defensive posture, including retention positions.

- Stability: An awareness of where your feet land and how to maintain a solid "base" at all times are key to fighting effectively. There is no differentiation between a hand-to-hand fight, a gun fight, or a ground fight. Base is of paramount importance at all times and should offer the platform for both impact and resistance stability as well as rapid movement launch.
- Mobility: To maintain maximum mobility in all directions possible. This is founded in footwork. Again, no differentiation is made between types of fighting. Mobility is a principle you should aspire to adhere to at all times. No matter where you end up, if you lose mobility, your ability to attack or defend is greatly reduced or eliminated altogether.
- Advanced Safety: DO NOT ADD HARM. At no time should any task or movement place myself, my teammates or innocents unnecessarily in harm's way because of my actions. An example of this is muzzle control in chaotic situations: To be able to nearly unconsciously control your muzzle rapidly *in all actions.*

In training, I am able to demonstrate clearly how these elements apply across the board for effective attack, defense and safety to achieve greater principles. That is how we can check ourselves when training or practicing: by asking ourselves, does this movement or task adhere to the elements and principles? A perfect example of this is the stance, one of the first things we learn in class. Whenever someone passes a pistol class off as a "fighting" or "gun fighting" course, yet they teach that isosceles is acceptable, I disagree with both assertions. I very easily demonstrate how unstable the stance is for force contact. Side to side it is OK, but front to back you have nothing and are very easily pushed off balance. The conversation goes like this:

Me: "If you were going to punch someone, is this how you would stand?"
Class: "No."
Me: "If I was trying to punch you, is this how you would stand?"
Class: "No."
Me: "Is getting into a shooting engagement a fight?"
Class: "Yes"
Me: "So, if getting into a gunfight is still a fight, and it can definitely go hands on or present a need to absorb impacts, and you would not stand in isosceles in a fist fight, why would you stand in isosceles in a fight? It's still a fight and anything can happen."

The point is that we are building our training from day one, lesson one, on the foundational principles of fighting. We are training to fight. Some things work great for other types of shooting, like isosceles and competition shooting. However, in fighting, it just does not pass the tests of strength, stability, mobility, time and efficiency. You can't absorb front or back impact without losing balance. You cannot deliver momentum or force with any effectiveness. You are only stable and mobile side to side. You lose time and efficiency by having to reposition your feet to move quickly forward or backward, or to absorb or deliver force. It is simply not a fighting stance. It violates the principles of fighting by forfeiting the elements of fighting adaptability. End of debate.

If I am forced into a fight, then my job is to begin and end that fight in a strong fighting position. *Everything I do is to improve my own position while worsening my opponent's position.* This should be cultivated right from the start and maintained by not doing things that violate the principles of strength, stability and mobility. Too often in our business the tendency to look fancy or to

59

look tactical or aggressive will far outweigh the need to actually stick to fighting principles.

Now, to hurt some more feelings, another great example of this is high pectoral index retention shooting. In all of my years of fighting, training and watching others get into fights never have I ever encountered a fighter or a style that believed placing the hand against the pectoral with the elbow high and way behind the body, extending the shoulder to its maximum extension of travel, was in any way an advantageous position to fight from. In fact, the ONLY time I have seen the arm in that position is when it is getting a kumora performed on it. A simple personal rule for me is that if it is not a position that I would put my body into during a close fight, then I will not use it during a close gunfight. It violates stability and mobility because it alters your base away from a natural fighting position and brings you closer into your attacker (assuming you are not shooting an unarmed attacker; he has a weapon to avoid).

Also, in order to have the muzzle on the enemy you must be closer to squared up, which creeps closer to that isosceles stance and lacks stability and mobility and brings your vital organs closer to a weapon wielding assailant. It also violates time and efficiency because there is absolutely zero accuracy reliability or accountability with pec-thumb index. Without accuracy accountability you cannot be efficient in the delivery of force, which may extend the fight beyond it's necessary length and expose you to more risk. If you land a few hits in the legs or abdomen, that guy can have a lot of fight left in him. If he then gets a hand on your gun, which is very possible, you will begin grappling from a position of weakness. Not to mention, I have not seen an example of it ever being used. Not in surveillance videos of real shootings, not in force-on-force training videos, and never in a fight first-hand.

I've tested this idea out by starting the grappling from both positions, the pec-index, and the strength elbow-to-ribcage position, with both gun students and with grappling practitioners who aren't shooters. The strength triangle is always stronger to

60

fight from. Remember, retention shooting doesn't mean the fight stops when the shots go off. This is the difference between retention shooting and weapon retention. Very often, the fight will *start* there. There are some simple tests to perform to see what produces the best results for both weapon retention capabilities in the upper body and for keeping a strong base during the fight. I have performed these tests with many skeptics and typically the results are evident that you can control the fight much better when you work from a fighting position and not an awkward position that extends a joint to its maximum travel to begin from.

As a fighter, being asked to do something outside of the mechanical advantage in a close fight is *no bueno* for me. As the elbow travels away from the body, in *any* direction, we lose strength *and* our base changes in how it will react to pressure. Perhaps there is a disconnect between the meanings of retention shooting vs weapon retention. If you believe your shots will blow the bad guy off his feet and vaporize him immediately, then a shooting position is a final destination and you need not worry further. However, if you believe, quite accurately, that gunshots don't always end the fight (Google "Jared Reston shooting") then you know that you will have to adhere to the principles of fighting throughout the fight including the positions you train to shoot from.

Now, to be fair, if the pec-thumb index turns out to be the only position I have to shoot from in a fight, you bet your ass I'll use it. It WILL work in limited circumstances against low-order attackers. But that is also because I believe and teach that you should be able to effectively run your gun no matter what position you find yourself in. Find a way to put rounds into the target, it's that simple. But I personally will not train a compromised position as a go-to position.

I'm sure the hate mail will flow about this. I am not here to change anyone's mind who isn't looking for a solution. I personally believe that a real close fight shooting situation will unfold without the use of any prescribed or rehearsed shooting method. Fights just do not look anything like the practice on the square range. What I attempt to convey is the adherence to basic fighting principles and elements no matter what the circumstances are, like maintaining strong positioning and allowing the freedom of footwork (mobility) to be an option. Attackers are not "compliant" and you can't just open yourself up on one side to perform a move on the other side, they will punish that opening. Most of the times I see things like "retention shooting" practiced or drilled, it appears as if the opponent is unarmed; there is no active threat being dealt with as far as a weapon in his hand, etc.

In other words, "retention shooting" is a bullshit gimmick taught on the square range to fill a perceived need that is not evidence based. It looks cool and boosts the attractiveness of a class. However, close fighting is a real thing. So, people do need to begin to think about operating with a gun in a close fight. At that point, it becomes a weapon of opportunity, not one of technique. If you have your solution that's great. If isosceles and high pectoral are in your playbook, then I hope it works for you and my feelings aren't hurt by what you think. As someone who has actually done a good amount of fighting in close, with deadly weapons, I'm comfortable with what I think works independent of what *an industry* thinks.

I am attempting to illustrate that there are very simple principles based on physics and human capability that can be adhered to in much stronger ways, and that these ways have been worked out in fighting systems for thousands of years. I have, in fact, fought over weapon retention several times, both over my own weapon and to attempt to take one away from someone else. This is where *my* opinion comes from. If you've fought over deadly weapons several times and have a unique experience, great. If you haven't fought over deadly weapons several times, then your opinion is simply theorized and/or adopted, so keep that in mind. While most of those fights with me involved knives, which are sharp and therefore much harder to grab and fight over, the principles still apply with the gun. Whatever you choose to use is 100% your decision, just make sure you can explain more than just "why" you use it. A "why" is not enough; we must have applicable principles to test the "why" against.

PRINCIPLE BASED TRAINING

The more fundamental a principle is, the more it will universally apply across the board. Principle based training is quite different than technique-based training. It's the difference between learning and mastering "moves" that are situation specific vs learning "why" things work in specific situations enough to understand how to transpose them into new and even untrained situations.

A good example of this happened when students took note of the similarities between my teaching and my grappling instructor's teaching at a particular class one day. For this class, the "Gutter Fight", I split the students into two groups. One group stayed with me for the combative section and the other group went with the grappling instructor. Eventually the group switched so everyone had the opportunity to work with both of us. When the exercise was finished everyone reconvened back in the classroom where a student commented on how much he liked how the coaches had made the lessons fit together and how each lesson enhanced the other perfectly.

This was a perfect teaching moment. I responded by saying, "That's funny, because I have no idea what Shane (my grappling coach) taught you guys." It was true. Shane and I had worked together before when I had my gym open. I know that Shane fully understands the principles of fighting and that he knows the goal is always to improve your position while worsening the enemy's. I fully trust that whatever he shows will adhere to the principles of strength, mobility and stability. Therefore, we had zero discussion before the class outside of me telling him to work about two solutions for a standing clinch fight. The end result was that we taught the students to attack the same points on the enemy without pre-planning because the principles of a clinch

63

fight do not change according to style or technique. The principles of fighting are independent of all of that. In fact, it is the requirement of styles and techniques to adhere to them, not the other way around. The students got two totally different viewpoints of attacking the same areas in different ways, and everything was based upon principles.

Principles require a deeper understanding to grasp. Most of the ancient fighting texts are more philosophical in context because they are strongly based on principles, especially those from the samurai lineage. The reason for this is simple: to become a truly accomplished fighter you must become fluid with your environment. In order to achieve this, an intuitive understanding of *how things work* must become natural to the fighter. Instead of being required to search through a catalog of moves to respond to his environment, the principle-based fighter intuitively understands time, efficiency, strength, mobility and stability and can apply them to any unfolding situation, independent of circumstance, allowing him to maintain the principles of control and adaptability. Principle based instruction transcends the restrictions of both styles and systems and the restrictions of each individual's unique way of learning. In the book, Learning and Understanding: Improving Advanced Study of Mathematics and Science in U.S. High Schools (2002), the authors laid out seven principles of "learning with understanding."

1. Learning with understanding is facilitated when new and existing knowledge is structured around the major concepts and principles of the discipline.
2. Learners use what they already know to construct new understandings.
3. Learning is facilitated through the use of metacognitive strategies that identify, monitor, and regulate cognitive processes.
4. Learners have different strategies, approaches, patterns of abilities, and learning styles that are a function of the

interaction between their heredity and their prior experiences.

5. Learners' motivation to learn and sense of self affects what is learned, how much is learned, and how much effort will be put into the learning process.
6. The practices and activities in which people engage while learning shape what is learned.
7. Learning is enhanced through socially supported interactions.

This is the key difference between learning with circumstance vs. learning with understanding, which equals the ability to apply knowledge to new situations based on learning that occurred under different circumstances. Principles reach across the divisions of styles, techniques, participant backgrounds, and the different ways that people learn.

Training systems inevitably move towards being complex and technical. This happens for several reasons. First, if all you did was teach the fundamentals over and over there will be a cap on how much money you will make because it's quite monotonous. People want fun, flashy, cool, and something that shows rank. Recently, the current trend is to want "scientific" and intricate sounding taxonomies. Second, in the vacuum of non-violence, because the training is art or sport and not real violence, the "style" is free to grow and be creatively expanded as it becomes further and further removed from the real world of violence. It literally never has to be tested against actual violence. This is great for an art or a sport, but not so much for individual or even team preparing for real fighting.

The most efficient violence I have ever witnessed was the highly developed predatory system of violence inside of prisons. A majority of the most effective and efficient killers are inside of those walls. Again, if you think that special operations military guys are the only (or most) efficient killers out there, you need to watch some documentaries on prison violence. I'm not saying special operations guys aren't good, I am saying that the truly violent predator has mastered doing it with very little equipment and very simple methods. Those tools and methods are based on adhering to fundamental principles. The only two places that real violence can repeatedly be found is in war, and in the criminal culture (especially prisons). Both are an unbroken lineage, and both are very different. What works in war does not so much apply to what works in prison, or in a parking lot by yourself on a dark night. Likewise, the other way around, what works on these streets in typical scenarios here would not apply as much in a war theater. Adherents to "training systems" need to keep this in mind when thinking about the applicability of their craft in real violent situations. The simplicity of the felonious killer cannot be overlooked. That simplicity is something that will work in interpersonal violence regardless of setting because it is based on fundamental principles.

The point I am driving at is that simplicity and fundamentals are reliable. They are reliable across situations and across circumstances. What doesn't work in war is specific to another circumstance, and vice versa. But if you begin to simplify your training to the fundamental principles, your knowledge becomes more universally applicable and much less circumstantially dependent.

WHAT IS *ADVANCED* TRAINING?

Before we talk about advanced training, let's define what fundamentals are. A fundamental is a central or primary rule or principle on which something is based. In training, fundamentals are often referring to basic skills. To understand how the word fundamental is appropriate in this way, we must see that the complex tasks involved in techniques, procedures and tactics are based upon central principles of basic skills. Therefore, fundamentals are the absolute foundation for everything you will do that is skill, technique or procedure based. As fundamentals become ingrained, there are then subsequently more complex tasks that need worked on in training. The best indicator that you are ready for advanced training is when you know you have reached **the point where basic fundamentals are repeatable enough to begin to reliably execute more complex tasks with them**.

Advanced training is taking the highly-trained and effortlessly repeatable fundamentals and stacking them together with other variables to create more complex tasks while processing the information coming at you in real time. This is where we develop both a very personalized technique and where we begin to understand and employ *procedures*. People fall into trap of thinking that shoothouse or close quarters fighting courses are inherently where all training leads to. Advanced has less to do with plate carriers and running and gunning than it has to do with being able to "stack" fundamental skills into more complex decisions and actions without using conscious brain resources. The gear and tactics part is purely determined by your mission (e.g. the likely scenarios you will face in the course of your daily life.) While many today will look at breach and clear or "run and gun" training and call it "advanced", I assert that it should be considered "specialized" training intended for specific jobs. Advanced has more to do with where YOU are at in your performance and what YOUR mission calls for, than it does with what particular actions you are doing or what you are wearing while you are doing it.

Too many people make the mistake of thinking that training is a linear, numerically defined progression. Although there may be a "Pistol 1, 2 and 3", it does NOT mean that you simply progress through them and you know the material or have the skills. The repeated practice and positive reinforcement of the fundamentals is the important part of the conditioning process. Without repetition, you will not retain or progress. I can teach you, but you must do it, to be able to do it. The majority of my regular students have taken my courses multiple times and return to take them each year. One reason is because you will never get exactly the same course. You are different, your skills change, the class has its own skill level collectively. There are many reasons that each class experience will be positive and will give you something to take away. This goes for taking fundamentals courses from other quality instructors as well.

Repeating courses is so important because *positive feedback reinforcement during effective practice* is important. So, while it is highly recommended that you venture out and train with multiple teachers to broaden your knowledge and skill set, if you are lucky enough to find an affordable and repeatable *home school* to train with, you need to capitalize on that as well. Most of all, you need to be able to take everything you learn and continue to *train yourself* going forward. People tend to think of military or law enforcement tactical training as "advanced" in that it is somehow inherently the natural progression of all training. It is not.

I see it more as a specialized training, but it is advanced in that you must be able to perform fundamental skills in combinations simultaneously while also not clogging up your mental resources so that you can process the room coming at you in real time. You can achieve the same level of performance in training that pertains to your civilian mission as well. The moral of the story is that all training, even advanced training, is (or should be) fundamentals. To what extent you can perform them on-demand without conscious processing determines the capability you have to synthesize new information as it comes in.

Are you training to think, or simply learning choreography?

Fighting effectively requires thinking. It is much more about rapid decision making than it is about punches, chokes and quick draws. Dozens of decisions can be made in the span of a few seconds, and in a lethal force conflict those decisions could mean the difference between living or dying. Are you training to make those decisions? Or, are you pre-programming yourself with choreographed moves that look good on social media? How do you know the difference?

Having known not only violent conflict but also violent people, I learned early on that things will become unpredictable with blinding speed. Some people are hard as hell to stop and may require constant attention beyond what you expected. Bystanders can suddenly run into your field of fire, or they can become assailants in a flash when their homie is losing to you. Anything can happen. You can end up with your back against a wall, in a strange parking lot, or be forced to fight from your vehicle. You may immediately need to evacuate your children or spouse from the area before anything else. You just do not know until you process the information coming at you in real time.

One technique or tactic is not going to work in every situation. Makes sense, right? So why would you train to do one single thing every single time you perform a certain task in training? Yes, there are certain things you do repeat until they become second nature: draw stroke, sight alignment, trigger pull, second sight picture…these are fundamentals. Fundamentals win fights. What I am talking about when I say choreography are things like stepping 12 inches before you shoot, shaking your head side to side to check your area, or turning a complete 360 after every shooting drill. (Ah yes, I can feel the hatred burning already from those who will defend these "tactical" rituals to the death.)

Before you lose your mind, let me say that every one of those techniques are legitimate. You need to know them and be ready to use them. But not one of them applies every time, so I do not support practicing them without assessment and decision. For example, if you have fought your back to a brick wall and you finish the fight with that wall at your back, what purpose does turning a complete 360 serve at that point? I know it sounds ridiculous to use such a simple example, but it's what comes to mind when I read the sensational internet debates on tactics and whole schools of instructors' minions that exist to preach the *one true way of the 360 no matter what.*

Some really teach that *no matter what,* you end every drill like this, because you "live in a 360-degree world." Bullshit. I've

69

been backed into more than one concrete corner in scary situations when my entire world was only 90 to 180 degrees and full of problems. Why don't you just use common sense when training and learn how to think all of the time, not just when you perceive circumstances to be appropriate for thinking. Because the real problem is the fact that you *will* perform what you have practiced in most circumstances. Every second in a deadly fight is an appropriate time for thinking, and think you must, if you want to stay alive and out of trouble.

Another one of my favorites is the step and draw. In a gunfight with a typical bad guy, the bad guy will most often be throwing bullets in your general direction and you have as much of a chance of stepping into a bullet as you do stepping out of the way of one. I've heard other smart instructors teach this, and I agree. Your mission is to remain unhurt while you put positive hits on the bad guy. Positive hits on the target is what will stop the fight. You can try to outrun the shooter, or you can stop the shooter. Stepping 12 inches will not outrun the shooter's line of fire. Hell, if you ran as fast as you could laterally you could not outrun his muzzle sweep. You run 12 feet, the shooter only has to move his muzzle 12 inches to cover you on that entire distance. (Exact numbers depend on how far away you are, but you get the idea.)

Sometimes it's what you need. Sometimes it's not. To test this out, have the most inexperienced person you know stand 15 feet away and point their "finger gun" at you. Now, quickly step one step to the side. Was it that difficult for their finger to stay on you? No. It's about a few inches of movement for them, and it's actually pretty natural for their finger to follow you. It's just ludicrous to think you can side step out of the path of a shooter who is tunnel-vision fixated on YOU. Especially when most criminal shooters are trigger-jerking idiots and will canvass your general area with bullets. The point is, if you are going to move, then MOVE. Don't half-ass it.

How about that side-to-side scan that looks so cool after some rapid-fire shots? This is an excellent example that I really want to twist those brain cells about. What are you really looking at? You do it "because I am training to always scan my area…" OK. But first, too often, you aren't scanning. No. You are not. I've watched countless people practice this on the range and, based on what I see in practice, it's a dance move. Theatrics in action. You are training yourself to make the physical movements, shaking your head side to side, but are you actually looking around? Can you run back a detailed checklist of what you actually looked at or saw taking place? You can? Then what the hell are you looking at in the 24" wide shooting stall shrouded by black ballistic walls on each side of you at your indoor range? Nothing. You are training yourself to look at nothing. And when the fight comes, that is exactly what you will see. You are being ridiculous by looking at absolutely nothing. In the spirit of adhering to the martial principles of time and efficiency, if there is nothing to look at, don't waste time looking at it.

Here's an example of what I am pointing out here. I have a ritual before I leave my house. Check my daily carry contents: gun, keys, wallet. Check to make sure lights are all off. Check the stove in case I forgot to turn it off. The other day, I reached my back door and remembered to check the stove. I walked through the house, into the kitchen, stopped, did an entire 360 scan, and headed back to the back door. Once at the back door, I realized that I did not see a damn thing I looked at. I went in and performed the motions. I pointed my head in all the requisite directions, but I could not tell you one thing I looked at, including whether the damn stove was left on or not. I was probably thinking about work, or the upcoming training session, who knows. I was performing a choreographed dance move with no real substantial effect. I had to go back to the kitchen and do it right. Over-practicing that one move—the side to side scan—will end with the same result. A mindless performance of a physical movement with very little real tactical application as it is practiced.

But the lack of actually looking at your area during a scan is not the biggest problem that I have observed with this move. The major flaw that I see taking place in training with the side to side scan is that it, in and of itself, becomes as important as the shot is to the shooter. What this results in is the shooter becomes anticipatory of the scan so much that they are working hard to get to the scan as the conclusion of a shot sequence. Why is this a problem? Because you are snatching your gun into chest ready and whipping your sights off of the target with no real process of confirming the target does not need more attention. In fact, getting that "second sight picture" isn't even practiced. The awesome looking side to side scan *is more important than the fight* is to you. The target and immediate area are not muzzle-scanned (checked through your sights) at all. BOOM-BOOM BOOM-SNAPBACK-SCAN SCAN!! In 95% of the practice I see, the last shot is fired and instantaneously the gun is whipped back into the chest as the head is already beginning the scan. As I stated before, sometimes a bad guy is hard to stop and will take more attention than you planned on using. And, sometimes you miss! In a real conflict situation where you've obviously been threatened enough to have to resort to deadly force on a target, you need to ensure that the problem is solved before you move on to your next move. The rule that I teach is, **if it's important enough to shoot, it's important enough to make sure it's shot!**

If you're going to practice the side to side scan, at least give yourself the training to ensure that the problem you just engaged is SOLVED before you move on to other things. Check your work through your sights, muzzle scan your target and ensure it is stopped. Muzzle scan with sights on the target, if something needs attention all you will need to do is apply pressure to the trigger. Once the problem is solved, move on to the next appropriate movement. This sounds like a lot, but only takes a fraction of time to perform. And the most needed action following a shot *may not be a scan*, it may be a *get the hell out of there NOW!* move. It may be get to the clear cover available to your right, or left, or behind you. It may be immediate evacuation of children from a dangerous death scene. Work your area on the way out.

So, what do you train to do? All of the above techniques and more. When someone asks me on the range what should I do after a shot my first absolute response is, *"Second sight picture. If the problem was serious enough to shoot at, it's serious enough to make sure it's shot. After that, you do what needs done when it needs done."* That could be a quick scan, a quick movement in any direction, a quick corralling of family away from the area...it's a dynamic world. Train to assess and react, not to simply act without thinking. The ability to process information, prioritize tasks, and react accordingly are the goals of training. Training should be about thinking your way through a fight, not choreography. Which brings us to the differentiation between kata training and fight training.

KATA BASED TRAINING VS FIGHT TRAINING

Everything works, if done at the right time.
Even the greatest technique fails, if done at the wrong time.

There are two types of people who train and teach in combatives: those who have actually done enough of the fighting to have the type of experiential knowledge that produces true confidence, and those who have only *trained* to fight. The problem with the training world is that the great majority of instructors out there have never really done it. Narrow that down even further if we want to talk about the narrow lane of criminal level violence (*which is what we are all training for, right?*). This isn't a problem because they don't know what they're talking about. No, there is a lot that you can learn from a dedicated student of violence or a martial art and there are plenty of instructors who've never been in a fight but have tons of good information.

The problem is that the culture, beliefs and norms of the combatives training world is shaped by the majority, and the majority are NOT experienced. They have pretended to fight for many years, but there is a key piece of the knowledge that cannot be replaced in the absence of having actually thrashed around in the blood and aftermath of deadly interpersonal violence. In this *training-only* environment, priorities get out of order.

For example, an experienced fighter can often recognize the experience level of another fighter by what he or she prioritizes in order of importance. If you, as a firearms instructor, are all about flash and fast draws, and allow that to dominate 90% of your curriculum, and never or rarely talk about footwork or decision-making, I will most likely categorize you as inexperienced unless you have something to prove otherwise. Flash and speed are important, but they are secondary--by far--in importance to confidently staying on your feet and thinking clearly. Staying on my feet and thinking clearly kept me alive several times. Literally. Far more times than any fast or fancy move.

So, I will emphasize that in my own course instruction. One of the results of this *training-only* dominated combatives culture is that training becomes driven by training. What this means is that instructors are 25 degrees removed from an actual experienced teacher, and as that information flows through the community it becomes dogma by rote, or what I like to refer to as kata based gunfight training. It becomes regurgitated information rather than *experienced, then shared,* information. Movements become more like choreography than actual fight skills. This becomes a kata; easy to copy and repeat and pass on. It's essentially a dance move, as it is taught and received. This happens because the techniques remain isolated katas, and conditioning is not taught, which would allow the student to OWN the technique.

The word "kata" (Japanese) classically referred to as a series of movements or a technique in a repeatable form for practice and repetition. Mainstream America was introduced to the kata during the kung-fu karate craze which swept the nation during the 1970's. (Who remembers Kung Fu Theater?) Suddenly, everyone and anyone could earn a black belt and be a badass like Chuck Norris. Just learn and memorize a series of movements and techniques, and perform them against semi-compliant opponent doing the exact same techniques under a set of rules, and all that black belt badassery was yours.

Less rules, more tools

The bluff was called in the 80's/90's when MMA came on the scene and "black belts" everywhere had their dreams crushed in the ring when their kata based fighting didn't pan out against the dynamic flow of someone with *less rules and more tools*, so to speak. For many reasons, kata based training was extremely ineffective for preparing them to face opponents who did not follow the same styles, forms or rules that they had trained for their whole careers. Of course, Brazilian Jiu Jitsu then dominated the martial arts scene and in many ways still does, yet many BJJ schools fail to differentiate between traditional BJJ and actual street fighting, leaving individuals with a false confidence that they are prepared for a mission that they never trained for. (Even the Gracie's themselves explain why most BJJ schools are NOT teaching street-ready BJJ. Search for "Street Jiu-Jitsu Vs Sport Jiu Jitsu" on the GracieAcademy channel.)

Gunfight training has unfortunately followed the way of the karate dojo and the sport BJJ schools in many ways. Many classes I personally have attended are nothing more than the teaching and repetition of katas, with no real context on how to progress as a fighter. Fast draws, side-to-side scans, side steps, touching the head while retention shooting...all taught with no intention of actually building the conditioning to perform the movements effectively and efficiently in real-time *as the result of real-time decision making.*

With the majority of instructors coming from training without the fighting background, gunfight training is overwhelmingly based on katas and sport. Typically, the student of such a shooting instruction system neither understands nor pursues the strength, speed or endurance to perform the movements they are learning. Learn the isolated movements, get fast at them, and achieve marksmanship worthy of a Facebook video and you've arrived. It's not that katas are inherently bad, as they do have some merit. The problem however is that our society has taken the "kata model", applied it to gun fighting (and everything else combative) and basically skipped the real work of conditioning.

Conditioning is what builds true capability. Conditioning is the only path to self-awareness and the development of naturally occurring technique. I have personally met several black belts who had zero conditioning work to go with that belt. If they were to get into a real fight, if a fancy move doesn't work within the first 30 seconds they are going to be sucking wind in a very serious way very quickly. But another very important side effect that lack of conditioning has is the practitioner never develops their own efficiencies and techniques. That innate ability to intuitively understand their own body and how to counteract their environment just never gets developed.

The emphasis becomes too often put on the *perfection* of a movement independent of outside variables. People really believe, and teach, that this is the pinnacle of accomplishment in fight training. It is not. It's only a beginning. The one who merely perfected a predictable movement in a predictable environment will lose. Having practiced a freestanding draw stroke to "perfection" won't help you when you are facing a hands-on attack and embroiled in a clinch fight (just one example). The one who is truly conditioned according to the principles of fighting, and of what the real goal is (*capabilities applied throughout adaptation to changing variables*), will observe, assess, correct and adapt.

Naturally occurring technique is the only technique that you truly own, since it was not taught to you exclusively, but is born of your efforts and growth in capability and understanding of effectiveness and efficiency. This type of naturally occurring technique only occurs through dedicated conditioning work. I have watched this happen not only on the range, but innumerable times in the fitness and fighting gyms that I worked in (and owned) for years.

Someone who never fought, punched, kicked or had any understanding on how to balance and leverage their own body will always begin in a very awkward way. They will appear very uncertain and clumsy. However, I would tell new members to just

76

do the bag work, help them with their punch technique to keep them safe, and let them go. Within weeks the ones who put the work in would begin to look more natural and confident on their feet without exclusive guidance in footwork. It just naturally develops. As a teacher I became aware that it is at this precise point that the student is very receptive to footwork because they now have a physical understanding of what you are trying to tell them about weight shifting, power production, etc., because they are naturally already doing it.

So, to make a great example, I personally emphasize footwork on the range in gunfight courses. I emphasize it because it is absolutely a priority to stay on your feet and win the fight, but also because it is overlooked, misunderstood and or completely skipped in 98% of the gunfight training out there now. The reason is because footwork is not kata based; in order to understand its importance and how it works well enough to teach, you have to have done it. Since footwork is not a natural component of gunfight training traditionally, if you have not been exposed to it through boxing or actually fighting, there really has been little opportunity to have come into contact with it. Yet, because fighting involves leverage and movement, stability and mobility, and can go hands on anytime, footwork is the foundation of the gunfighter just as much as it is the foundation of the boxer. It's not kata based, and it can only be developed through conditioning. Like footwork, there are many components of fight preparation that kata based training will always miss.

Standing on a range and doing a prescribed movement can have its benefits, but you must know that once the fundamentals are in place it's time to work hard and develop technique through true ability. That can only be produced through conditioning work over sustained periods of time. Some skills and types of knowledge cannot be taught, bought or gifted. It has to be earned through a deep and intuitive understanding of the underlying principles. Advanced fighting skill is unarguably in that category.

Conditioning develops the speed, strength and endurance for the physical performance. Conditioning allows technique to naturally occur in a way the fighter truly OWNS. Conditioning improves performance. Improved performance increases confidence.

Conditioning strengthens the Orientation through psychological confidence. Confidence is the most important component of Orientation to combat uncertainty. Uncertainty is the enemy of every fighter.

CHAPTER SIX: SKILLS, TECHNIQUES, PROCEDURES, TACTICS AND STANDARDS

SKILLS

Skills training is first and foremost in the actual physical training of a fighter. Your basic, fundamental skills MUST be mastered first before you can progress to any other tasks. The reason for this is because your more complex tasks are built from these fundamental skills. Let me repeat that, *your advanced or complex tasks are built from your fundamental skills!* Therefore, if one or more skills are performed incorrectly, you will stack mistakes on top of mistakes as you begin to combine skills with other skills and do them incorrectly.

In other words, look at moving while drawing and shooting. Do you know how to run? Do you know how to draw your weapon safely and effectively? Do you know how to shoot while moving? Do you know how to control your muzzle during this series of events? Do you know how to account for terrain differences, obstacles, other people, etc. during this series of events? Each one of those questions is asking for a specific basic skill: running; draw stroke; shooting; muzzle control; situational awareness; etc. Combining them and adjusting them within the demands of the situation then becomes advanced technique and procedure. Any one of them may not be a big problem to accomplish flawlessly. However, begin stacking them together and things can get pretty complicated. It requires you to not only be able to perform each skill well, but to be able to perform them together when you cannot possibly give your focus to any one of them individually. Keep in mind that during this performance we must maintain adherence to the martial principles discussed earlier so as to minimize our risk. This is a tall order. Thus, we begin the process of learning the fundamentals and ingraining them to the point of automaticity.

THE MODEL OF COMPETENCE BASED PERFORMANCE

There is a very popular learning model often referred to as the "conscious competence learning matrix" that depicts the stages of learning and competence in skills performance. It is arguable who originated the theory, and there have been several variations since its widespread use in the U.S., beginning in the early 1970's. For our purposes, I will present a general version:

- Stage 1: Unconscious Incompetence
  - The student is not aware of particular skills or knowledge at all
  - The student is not aware that they have a deficiency in the skills and knowledge
  - Condition is often protected by denying that the skills or knowledge are even important or needed
- Stage 2: Conscious Incompetence
  - The student gains awareness of the skills and knowledge
  - The student is aware of their deficiency in the skills and knowledge
  - The student is aware of the importance of the skills and knowledge
- Stage 3: Conscious Competence
  - The student can perform the skills at will reliably, but still has to think about it and focus to perform well
  - The student understands the importance of the skills and their performance and puts in the requisite practice to maintain capabilities
- Stage 4: Unconscious Competence
  - The skills become natural and can be performed *without focusing and thinking about them directly*

(many of the skills of driving a car are good examples of this)
- o The student has practiced and repeated the skills so much that they don't even have to manually recall and decide to use the skills, the brain will run the skills as a default program when the need arises, and the student may not even be aware fully that they performed the skills.
- Stage 5: Retrospective Articulation
    - o The practitioner is not only able to thoughtlessly perform the tasks without focusing and thinking about the performance. They can also look back retrospectively and examine then explain what they did, how they did it, and why it worked that way.

Unconscious Incompetence

Stage 1 is the hardest one we fight against in the firearms community. There is nothing as impenetrable as the belief that simply being exposed to and/or shooting guns makes you competent. If you doubt people think this way, go work in a gun store for a short time. There is a tremendous amount of people who own guns that legitimately believe that an NRA basic pistol course at a gun club is representative of everything that firearms related training has to offer. I would even go further and say that a majority of average gun owners may believe that. That belief is definitely an example of unconscious incompetence. Because they are not truly aware of what is out there, they deny it's importance if you try to explain it. Unconscious incompetence all too often is accompanied by an unwillingness to listen. And, sometimes, there is just no fix for that.

Getting yourself or someone, else past unconscious incompetence requires, at some point, listening to the possibility of something greater. You must be ready to accept that maybe there is more out there than you are aware of, and that it is very important information to should know. The first step out of that state of ignorance is the acceptance of the ignorance or lack of

81

capability. I loved one aspect of teaching basic concealed carry courses when I used to do a lot of them, and that was watching unconscious incompetence fail on the range. By safely allowing their belief system to fail, repeatedly, they are left with little argument to continue to embrace it. Learning can occur; if only through failure sometimes.

Conscious Incompetence

Stage 2 is where the student acknowledges a few things that are required for improvement to happen. First, they acknowledge that there are skills and knowledge out there, they acknowledge that the skills are important to the goals they have, and they also acknowledge that they have a deficiency in these skills. Acceptance is the first step, as they say. It is ONLY at this point that the student is ready to learn and will willingly receive instruction and or practice.

Conscious Competence

Stage 3 is the where the beginner begins to have some successes in skills performance. A key change here is that the student accepts and embraces the importance of the knowledge and skills. It is very important to note that no one will reliably retain information that they do not deem important (generally speaking). The more important someone deems a skill or piece of information, the higher the chance of them learning, retaining and practicing it. It's just a fact of adult learning. Therefore, in order to achieve the level of conscious competence, the student must first understand the importance of the skills, and next must practice the skills to be able to perform them.

At this stage, it still requires focus and thought to perform flawlessly. This means that the student is definitely not ready to begin stacking skill demands together, as we refer to advanced training. If it still requires concentration and thought to successfully perform isolated skills well, success will rapidly decline as skill demands become complex and stacked together all at once. The answer is to keep practicing and keep returning to train with someone who can offer positive feedback.

Unconscious Competence

This is where the skills become like what some refer to as "second nature". For the student/practitioner, this is the goal. If you train the skills properly enough times, you WILL reach a point where you will be able to perform the skills without actively concentrating on the performance of the skill. When you first learned to drive a car, you probably were not very skillful when it was time to accelerate or stop. I'm pretty sure all of us nearly gave our teacher whiplash the first time we stepped on the brake pedal. Today, I am confident that you probably step on the brake pedal so gracefully that you do it literally hundreds of times a week and do not even notice that you are doing it. That is unconscious competence at work. The skill is ingrained and so well practiced that you can not only perform it without focusing on it, but your brain can actually make the decision to employ the skill without your conscious, active attention to the decision-making process.

How did this happen? It was at first the realization that you weren't that good at it and that you really needed to be. Next, it was the repetition, over and over, just repeating the act until it became smooth. Smooth will become fast, if needed (but we'll get to that later.) The important point right now is to realize that unconscious competence is the result of proper practice. This is what instructors and teachers mean when they say that the fundamentals should be trained until they become automatic. I will say it again. It is my belief that the non-conscious performance of an individual cannot be taught, bought or gifted. You'll hear me say this repeatedly: training and conditioning around the fundamental skills will allow technique to naturally develop.

This is true. This is why we must move past the "kata" type training and move into conditioning around fundamentals. It is not the perfection of a movement that we seek. No. It is the capability to perform the movement and yet observe, assess, correct and adapt to any changes happening in your environment. Performing a movement perfectly under predictable conditions is not the pinnacle of accomplishment. Performing a movement correctly and effectively under unpredictable changes in variables and environment are the true mark of accomplishment in skill level.

The "Fifth Stage" Retrospective Articulation

There have been several suggestions for a "fifth stage" that is centered around articulation and teaching. It must be discussed as part of the continuum. The fact that skills become "automatic" inherently means that little concentrated thought is put into their performance. It has been argued that it seems impossible to articulate or teach something that you are not consciously making decisions about and performing. This can be true. I have met many people who are awesome at tasks, yet can't explain how they do it to save their life. If you are going to be a teacher, who is teaching from *experience*, you need to reach a fifth stage of reflective unconscious competence, and have the ability to analyze your skills and knowledge retroactively. I would also argue that there needs to be at least a minimum amount of this utilized for self-defense purposes, because post-event articulation is mandatory and may decide your future in very life changing ways. If you cannot explain what you did and why you did it, you may have some serious trouble.

One of the best ways to begin to learn how to articulate retrospectively is to stay within your mission. If you have trained hard in a system that is designed around your specific mission and specific parameters, then it is much easier for you to KNOW you have stayed within the boundaries and the "why" that caused you to engage in the fight. That can help with the legal articulation part of it.

To be able to teach the physical task is a different story. Retrospective articulation is going to require a pretty high level of understanding that you have developed through conditioning and experience. Your understanding of the principles of efficiency, time, movement, stability, leverage, as well as of the capabilities of your tools, will be where your skill set articulation comes from. If you cannot first intellectually understand why a certain task is both necessary and possible, you cannot explain it to anyone else. And you sure as hell cannot effectively teach that task in a way the student will develop their own articulation about it.. And if your students are not developing the articulation to explain why their skill sets are necessary, possible and legal, you are not teaching them self-defense.

On a mastery level retrospective articulation is more than just explaining to a court why you took the particular actions you did. That's really a byproduct of it. The real mastery of it is being able to both understand the principles behind your actions *and* explain them in a way that others could gain a fundamental understanding of them as well. When it comes to fighting and violence, those who do the real stuff learn by doing. Criminals learn by doing. So, there is a lack of contextual explanation to begin with. This is the reason why some of the most effective fighters have difficulty explaining how they can fight so well.

Take any good fighter and have them explain what to do in a particular fight scenario. Then, put them in a sparring scenario just like it and you will see them do things that they did not describe. Subtle moves, shifting of weight, anticipation of the opponent's movements, every good fighter has an entire toolbox of skills that are employed at the subconscious level; they do not consciously think about them, they just do them. This is what is hard to articulate. It is much easier to do if your entire skill set is gained and practiced in a controlled setting in a learning environment. Take the super technical jiu jitsu practitioner, for example. He will be able to articulate the subtle movements used to shift weight and gain position, etc., because he was taught that way, through articulation and demonstration. But when we are talking about raw violence, there exists no controlled setting to teach raw violence. The closest that exists to that setting is prison, and it is not learned through articulation and demonstration. There is some training, if you're lucky to have a mentor, or you roll with a gang, but the majority of the skill set is learned by conditioning and then doing.

It becomes clearer why it is apparent when someone talks about something that they haven't actually done when we think about this retrospective articulation. It can't be retrospective if you haven't done it, and there is nothing like information from someone who has been there. It's a reminder to be mindful of your skills as you condition and develop them. Pay attention to how your movement pathways change as you become more confident. Take note of how you are able to read another person in the ways that they shift their weight and move their feet. If you pay attention as these skills develop, you have a much better chance of articulating how it works later. I can remember fighting as a kid growing up rough and thinking very clearly during the fight about why something didn't work and how I could make it work, or find something else that works. This works equally well by watching what works for others and understanding the "why" behind it. Retrospective articulation begins with honest self-awareness, especially during stressful moments.

Slow is Fast?

We have talked about training the fundamentals until they are "automatic". We need to repetitively train the fundamentals until we can perform them, repeatedly, without having to think about them at a conscious level.

This is not accomplished by going as fast as you can from the very start. Have you ever taken a day and just went out specifically to practice slamming on your brakes in your car? Probably not. However, when the moment comes at 50mph and something goes bad in front of you, you will slam on your brakes with extreme unconscious competence and stop the vehicle. The reason you can achieve the brake pedal movement flawlessly is NOT because you have practiced slamming the pedal at that speed. It is because every week you have performed literally thousands of slow, correct repetitions of going from the gas pedal to the brake pedal.

If you train your fighting skills in the same slow, correct and deliberate manner, you will find that when speed is needed, *at a basic level* it will be there. Fast technique is a product of smooth and correct performance of repetitions *that is then applied with speed*. Smooth and correct essentially mean *efficient*. So, yes, you do have to go fast to go fast, it is nonsense to think otherwise. *But you can't go fast FIRST!* You have to start out by practicing, not necessarily slow, but smooth. Smooth and correct has to come first. Anyone who disagrees with this needs to prove it wrong by taking a series of *brand new* shooters, who have *never* performed a draw stroke, and show me how they will skip doing it slowly and correctly to just make them fast and accurate on the very first reps. It's impossible.

I know there is a growing trend in the industry to mock the "*smooth is fast*" mantra. Those mocking it are taking it out of context, in my opinion. It is easy to conclude that the words "slow" and "fast" are two different words that do not mean the same thing. Now, people are making the argument that "slow is smooth and smooth is fast" is "stupid because you can't go fast if you're going slow" Well, no shit. I don't think anyone thinks that always going slow means you automatically will go fast. We all know-- you guys who mock it included--that you do not take someone brand new to guns and shooting, hand them a gun for the first time and throw a timer on them with the demand to get the gun out as fast as possible and hit the target 7 yards away. It's unrealistic and unsafe to expect that performance from someone who has *never* done it. Going slowly in the beginning helps to understand and learn the mechanics necessary to perform faster. During this process, it is emphasized that one must be smooth and correct (efficient), and eliminate flaws and stutters, in order to develop the gliding pathways that speed requires.

Anyone who has trained up to the procedural level will recognize this immediately. Take CQB training, for example. When new trainees enter the shoothouse to learn standard operating procedures for processing doors, rooms and hallways, they almost always try to go fast. They are inevitably a shit-show of deficient performance. It takes consistent drilling over multiple days to get them to slow down and only move at a pace that they can begin to process what they are looking at.

In other words, do not move faster than you can process the information coming at you. Instead, whether it's because they want to be CQB gods, or they are just nervous, people speed up and then they screw up. With time they begin to SLOW DOWN, and thus become much smoother. *And then something magical happens*: **they are moving slower, but they are much faster through the procedures and through the house overall. They have created *momentum* by eliminating stutter and hesitation.** In CQB, slow is smooth and smooth is fast, and you can see it happen right before your own eyes.

John Chapman teaches that momentum has a huge role in winning CQB fights. I would agree that this is true in most violent engagements. Momentum, for this purpose, is defined as consistent pressure toward the enemy *without hesitations*; taking the fight to them without stutter. The way to accomplish this is by being smooth. You accomplish smooth by not going faster than you can process information in real time. Therefore, you slow down, you have less hesitations, and you become smooth. This creates momentum by reducing hesitation, and you overall become faster. It's that simple. While something like the draw stroke is a skill and CQB involves complex mental processing, CQB procedures are made up of basic skills like gun manipulation and marksmanship, movement, etc. So, it absolutely applies at the skill level.

It has been taught for decades, with remarkable success, that *slow is smooth and smooth is fast*. However, sometimes we can't have nice things because someone has to show how *smart* they are and put things down in a different context. We all know that slow and fast have two different meanings and are not the same thing. Arguing over semantics and interpretations of them is simply a waste of time. My answer to this (and my suggestion for you) is to simply find ways to convey the concept without using now controversial mantras. In all honesty, there are better ways to say it. I just wanted to point out here, from my perspective, that it really just means you cannot perform a smooth movement with speed if you cannot first perform a slow movement smoothly, correctly, and repeatedly. I still believe and teach this in skills level training.

Why speed becoming automatic is important

We know this is true because we do not go fast and think about what we are doing. When we get fast, it is automaticity at that point. For fighting, I preach skills to automatically because you need your processor resources to make decisions in real time. Improving the efficiency of your processor requires basic skills being ingrained enough to not have to use processor resources on them. Which allows you to then process information more quickly and thoroughly. This is the path to rapid and correct decision making in a fight. When you are not worrying about whether you can actually perform a movement or not, you are able to delegate those movements to the unconscious mind and allow your conscious mind to be fully engaged in the observance and decision-making processes.

As the skills become trustworthy, you can go straight to processing your environment. This is a good step, but there's more. The concept of maximizing your processor speed by not using resources thinking about the basics, allows you to not only solve one problem at a time, but to be able to flow through many problems, one after the other. It gets so good that you can set up subsequent moves with the ending of each solution. That is achieved after many, many hours of practice, force on force and mental training with positive mental imagery. Like shooting pool. First learn how to make the ball go into the pocket. With practice, we can make the ball go into the pocket with the cue coming to rest in position to make another ball go into a pocket... But for now, let's focus on practicing the isolated skill to reliable perfection.

Positive mental imagery plays a key role in keeping you on the quick end of the spectrum during practice. This is possibly the most difficult part of training: not picturing ourselves failing. We have to DENY those negative images from gaining entry. We have all stepped up to perform at some point in time and failed. Whether at the range, or in a sport, we feared failure at the critical moment before performance. When you fear failure, you will picture yourself failing. This image will bog down your processing speed and prohibit you from performing well. Denying these images of failure, and other fear based anxieties, from entering into your observance and decision-making processes will allow you to perform the fundamental skills necessary to prevail. It is truly difficult sometimes to imagine yourself doing something flawlessly correct, but it MUST be worked on. The faster we try to go, the harder it is to block out the imagery of failure IF we are still thinking about the performance. This is why speed and automaticity go hand in hand.

Is there a time when going slow will not propel you forward? The short answer is "yes". If you never test yourself or push yourself to go harder and faster, you simply can never count on being able to go harder or faster if you someday need to. However, pushing people to "just go fast" is the bullshit that supports famous social media, speed-shooters who pass themselves off as defensive fighters and instructors. Speed for the sake of speed is not sufficient. For the fighter, there needs to be a complete understanding of what it is we are actually trying to accomplish there.

Speed is a result of smooth and correct repetitious practice that creates the ability to perform movements without conscious intervention during the process. Anyone who has achieved a great level of speed will tell you that they are not "thinking" about the movements when they are doing them. They just do it. This allows them to use their conscious thought resources to focus on processing the information coming at them in the fight and to make quick, clear decisions, while simultaneously not over-thinking a given task and screwing it up. Simply jamming away on the range isn't going to make that happen. Do it correctly, frequently, and increasingly with more speed and less thought.

The importance of correct practice

Although I am aware of the science backing up what I have to say, this is as close as I will get to being scientific in this book. When we talk about practice, we need to immediately and forcefully kill the myth that "practice makes perfect". It simply is not true. Practice makes something reliably repeatable. But understand this very important fact: it becomes repeatable in the way that you have practiced it. FACT: *If you practice it wrong, you will get really good at doing it wrong.* This means, if you have made it a habit to try to go too fast, and to not seek out positive feedback, you may have actually practiced doing something incorrectly. The biggest cause of this that I see is going too fast. Remember what I said about the car brake pedal and hitting the brakes quickly? Practicing fast does not make you fast. Practicing smoothly and correctly, and *then* pushing your speed boundaries, makes you fast and correct.

Think of your neural pathways like weeds in the woods. If you want to make a new path in the woods, where it is all grown up with undergrowth, you have to walk that new path several times to even make it visible. As you walk the path for months over and over, eventually it turns into a recognizable clear path. This is just like the neural pathways that tell your muscles to fire in a certain pattern. As you practice, you are myelinating the axons, which speeds up the electrical signal across the neural pathway. This means the more frequently you practice, the faster you get at doing it exactly the way you practice.

So, again imagine you are going to cut a new path in the woods. However, this time, you walk a slightly different way each day and never walk over the same exact pathway twice. How successful do you think you would be at efficiently trampling the undergrowth down and making a visible, clear path? You wouldn't be. If you deviate each time, even slightly, you will not develop one well-worn path. Or, it will be a huge, sloppy path with spotty growth and obstruction here and there.

Your neural pathways can be viewed similarly. When we deviate our path of movement when practicing a skill, there is no way to efficiently train ourselves to perform it the one intended way. While it is ok to work into advanced levels where we train variants of a technique or skill on purpose, it can only be done after the basic primary skill has been perfected to an automatic, non-conscious performance ability. This is the primary reason for the methods that I use in my training classes.

The most common and pretty much expected mistake that I see newer students and shooters make is to begin pursuing speed much too soon in their training. Everyone wants to be Instagram hot and perform cool shit with the timer. But if you try to do this before putting your time in, as you speed up you begin to automatically cut corners, make mistakes, fumble tasks and just plain screw up. This is what you are practicing! *Every practice run that you fumble is a step backward in your training toward correct skill performance.* Resist the urge to always go fast. It is much better to *perform perfectly at whatever speed you can maintain perfect pathway performance* at. Save speed for testing and pushing boundaries. Remember the example of the brake pedal and your skill at emergency braking, without ever really practicing emergency braking? It is simply true that the slow, repeated perfect practice of a skill will program the brain and body to perform that skill on-demand and at greater speeds than practiced. Speed is for testing and fun, but do not make testing the majority of your time on the range. I say this because this is what I see most people do. Practice is for doing it perfectly correct. Do not forget this. Make this the cornerstone of your physical training protocol.

Note: I want you to keep something in mind here. I am talking about fight training. This matters because I am someone who has successfully done a lot of fighting and engaged in extreme violence. What I am telling you might not necessarily be the best path to some other goal, like competition shooting, or something else that is not actual fight training. I am conveying to you the reverse-engineered conditioning that I personally watched build many great fighters and very deadly people.

Footwork in fight training

FACT: Footwork is the absolute foundation of the fighter during a stand-up fight. Gunfights almost always start (and usually end) as stand-up fights. Being a former fighter, and having done a shit load of real fighting, I was blown away by the complete absence of footwork in 99% of the instruction I experienced in the gunfight training world. It amazes me that the very foundation of the fighter is just overlooked with complete abandon, when in the fighting world it is quite literally what everything else is based upon in your training. I mean, if we are going to take it literally that we are training to fight--with or without a gun--in self-defense, we MUST address the foundational problems of movement and stability during violence. It all starts with your *base*!

In my training classes on the range, I do footwork shooting drills that seem very simple at first. An example is a shooter moves forward 3 steps on command only: straight, diagonal right, or diagonal left. At the end of each movement, the shooter performs 2 or 3 shots on target. We begin at 25 yards. The rules are that you must not land with the same foot forward every time, the weapon stays on target, goes to "low ready", or "sol" position (depending on the purpose) during movement. A caveat is that the shooter must be moving if a reload is being performed. By using only 3 steps, the shooter should land with alternating feet forward each time. The directions are by command, so they are random and by surprise.

If you want to see adults glitch like video game characters and lose their ability to think and execute, this is a great drill for that. The first thing it does is shows they are not ready to perform multiple tasks with changing variables around them, and it begins to train the fighter to find a stable platform no matter where his or her feet land. Once a good stance is built, we have to then break our reliance on that *particular* stance and be able to find the principles of that stance in other positions.

This is very important because it breaks our reliance on a "perfect" stance and *trains the brain and body how to recognize and find its stability and mobility and keep them.* If you are engaging in a gunfight for self-defense, it is extremely possible that you will experience some type of contact. Without the ability to keep and maintain a solid base underneath you, your success will be seriously compromised if you are impacted by a round, rushed by the attacker, or smashed into by a panicking innocent trying to flee the scene.

Both stance and footwork should adhere to two principles:
1. We must have stability for force production, and resistance to impact, as close to 360 degrees around us as possible.
2. We must have mobility to move quickly in any direction as close to 360 degrees as possible *without repositioning our feet for a launch.*

So, any time you are practicing you can stop in place, look down, and ask yourself if you are violating either of those two principles. As an example, the isosceles stance violates both principles. While it offers great stability and mobility side-to-side, it offers no stability or mobility forward or backward. I always demonstrate this on the range when I ask students, first thing in the morning, to show me their shooting stances. Inevitably, someone is using isosceles and I bring them up front, get them in their stance, and then I push rearward on their imaginary gun (hands extended out in front of them). I tell them to get strong in their stance and then literally use one finger to push them off balance. Every time, they stumble rearward after the most minimal push against them. I then have them shift into a staggered foot position, more like a boxer's stance. I am unable to push them rearward using even more force than the first time.

Now, I am aware that it is literally impossible to maintain 360 degrees of true stability as a bi-pedal creature, only having two legs. However, the way we use our foot placement and hips to create the "X" across our center of gravity can create a responsive system of stability in our foundation that is capable of producing force and absorbing impact almost in any direction. This is what we strive for at all times.

Every home defense or CQB class I teach will include great shooters with terrible footwork. As they move through the shapes of a structure, they are clumsy, unsure on their feet, crossing legs and otherwise just repeatedly putting themselves in horribly weak and unstable positions. The more "cautious" they are being, the more prone they are to put themselves in these horribly weak positions. This means that nearly every time they approach an area that would pose the highest risk of encountering a sudden fight, they are getting weaker and weaker the deeper towards danger they go. In a home invasion situation, if you MUST move through the structure (meaning you have no other choice) then it is extremely likely that you could be in a force contact situation by surprise around any given corner. This is NOT the time to be caught standing like a rhinoceros in a tutu on the toes of one foot. Every step should be certain, when one foot is off the ground in movement, you are out of the fight to some degree. This is why boxers "glide" across the canvas, efficiency and time. Efficiency of movement and adherence to mobility and stability will minimize that time out of the fight. This is why those principles apply across the board, whether it's a boxing match, a gunfight in the parking lot, or a team doing entry and clearance of a structure.

Because footwork is what we need to be prepared to do, our stance is then built off of the demands of footwork. The stance is your starting point, should you get enough warning to even use a stance as a beginning. Like everything else, we don't do what feels best, or what I shoot best in, we do what is most effective, most efficient *and* what minimizes our time fighting. If I have to reposition my feet to launch into movement, it is not efficient. If I get knocked off of my base by a panicking runner, my time out of the fight is not minimized. If the fight goes hands-on and I don't have a solid base under me to position and leverage my force, I

95

am not effective or in the fight. I adhere to those two principles by making sure my stance and footwork adhere to the principles of stability and mobility at all times.

I am also a big fan of simplicity. The minimum number of variables and minimum number of steps you use, the less chance for things to get screwed up. When it comes to stance, I use the same stance for rifle, pistol and hand-to-hand fighting. It's so ingrained in me from years of training and fighting that I couldn't change it smoothly if I tried at this point. But training it that way has made life so much easier moving between weapon platforms and fighting styles. It also adheres to the same principles no matter what I am using in the fight. It just never made sense to me that so many people teach gun *fighting,* and openly acknowledge that gunfights can go hands on, yet not only do they NOT teach fighting stance or footwork they actually teach stances and movements that you most certainly would never do if you were actually training to be in a fight. This is the problem with the culture of training being controlled by trainees, and not fighters.

If you really want to get some footwork down and begin to understand what I am talking about here, go to a boxing coach for a little while. If you grapple, get off of your damn back and fight on your feet some. (For the love of Valhalla don't spend every fucking minute in the gym on the ground.) Or at least find some YouTube videos or get some DVD's on boxing footwork. Impact is impact, whether it's a punch in your face or the recoil of the weapon you are holding. Boxing footwork is a science to keep you on your feet while both delivering impact and absorbing impact, among other things. It greatly adheres to the stability and mobility principles. I'm not saying that boxing footwork is exactly what's needed in gun fighting footwork. What I am saying is that it's a great starting point for understand how to stay mobile and strong on your feet when engaged in battle. It's a great fundamental system.

TECHNIQUES

Techniques are variations on skills that adjust a skill to be more effective, efficient, safe or achievable to an individual and/or situation. Performing a draw stroke can be pretty straight forward. However, performing a draw stroke in close contact, while not muzzling your own body, will require adjustments and *technique*. As you can see, the basic skills need to be mastered first, before you can even think about developing technique. Having trained, fought and trained others for many years, I firmly believe that technique will largely emerge naturally from the proper dedication to training the fundamental skills (when coupled with physical conditioning.) As you grow confident and efficient in basic skills, you will begin to develop pathways and efficiencies *that adhere to the principles of the skill* while improving your performance and safety at the same time. This is technique.

Naturally occurring technique

I am a firm believer there is a dramatic difference between copying what you are taught, and truly performing it intuitively with your individual signature. That difference happens through dedicated conditioning work. I owned a conditioning gym for a while and I advertised it as "combat fitness". When people showed up, they imagined they would learn how to punch, kick and grapple. While we had some guest instructors come in and do sessions here and there on style and technique, the bulk of the program was just hard work on striking bags, rubber bands, full range of motion and explosive lifting, etc. (depending on experience level) all to a round timer for the duration of the session, which would be 2 to 3 hours; 2 minutes on, one minute off.

In the beginning, participants almost always run out of gas before 2 minutes is up on the first bag round, and would have a very slow pace to last maybe 45 minutes with a lot of standing around. Within weeks we watched participants build that stamina and before you knew it, the 54-year-old guy who hadn't worked out in years was slamming 30 rounds straight without even realizing he's an hour and a half into a blazing workout.

But the most interesting part is the emergence of technique in that process. My boxing coach used this method on me, and I adopted it and refined it over the 15 or so years I've been training people both on the range and in the gym. When I showed up for my first practice, the coach showed me *the minimum,* so I wouldn't break my hands or wrists on the bag or hurt myself. He just made me work. I thought, "this is bullshit! I came here to learn how to fight!" After a month or two of doing 40 rounds a day, 4 days a week, I became a monster. I literally felt like I could outrun a gazelle, jump over cars, and outlast 99.9% of the people on the street in a fight. But my technique emerged on its own. When it began to show up, that's when the coach stepped in and began to just refine me. It was brilliant. In one way, I earned the instruction and proved it was worth his time as a teacher as he vetted out the ones who just would not put the work in without an immediate reward. In another way, I made the technique my own.

This is exactly what I witnessed with my guys and girls in the combat fitness gym. In the beginning they were so awkward; didn't know where to put their feet, had very little power transfer capabilities; they just did not know how to use their own bodies. But if they put the work in, and just hammered it out, with enough guidance to keep them safe and away from bad habits, within weeks the transformation was amazing. The kinesthetic awareness alone can't be achieved any other way, and there is no way you will maximize efficiency and effectiveness if you do not intuitively understand how your body creates power and leverage.

Once this happens, then it's productive to begin force on force work, but not before, in my opinion. Testing skills should come later after some base level of ability and self-awareness is built. Throwing someone into the pit to grapple or spar too early can be damaging to their well-being and their progress if they are not guided into developing some confidence and technique that they really understand.

When I get students into a seminar or a weekend course, more often than not a good majority of them have no idea how to use their bodies to produce force or leverage, or how to seek the greatest positions of stability and mobility. Yet these same students will jump into sparring courses. While it's good to experience a scuffle, I believe you will get much farther if you learn the fundamentals of force production and stability first. Once you have conditioned with the fundamentals, technique will become clearer and its application in force-on-force will then be possible to a greater extent.

Technique is skill advanced to a personal level, unique to you. This ability is largely based on proprioception, or "The unconscious perception of movement and spatial orientation arising from stimuli within the body itself." It's a way we begin to accurately judge how far we have to move, how to shift our weight, etc. We all have this developed to a high degree already. I believe that this is what some people refer to (erroneously) as "muscle memory." When we walk, drive a car, open doors, etc. we are using developed proprioceptive awareness to efficiently execute the movements with accuracy and without much conscious thought. That proprioceptive awareness gives us an unconscious "kinesthetic sense" of where we are in space and where we may need to be.

At a basic level, it's how you know where your hands and feet are without having to look at them. Developing proprioceptive awareness can be greatly improved through repetition. This is what happened to the gym members that started out totally awkward and within a month or two are beginning to look natural in their movements. With guidance and feedback, we develop this awareness quite quickly. Whether you are training gun skills, combatives, or just functional, full range of motion capabilities you have to develop this proprioceptive sense to become effective at the development and application of your own technique. Too many people believe that rehearsing the kata over and over is a path to this. It is only a beginning.

In order to truly be able to own your technique and apply it independent of specific circumstances, you need to have a physical sense for the principles of movement. In doing so, you'll understand immediately, intuitively, how to adjust your movements to the demands of your changing environment. It's the development of technique on demand. By understanding the principles of fighting and having the proprioceptive sense developed to a high degree, you can easily translate skills learned while standing on your feet out in the open to suddenly working in a confined space such as a jail cell, an ambulance, or in a car. A draw stroke still requires you to get the gun out and towards the threat in the most efficient and safe manner possible. An underhook or joint lock still require you to establish a base, gain position, impose leverage, and apply pressure.

This is just a few paragraphs in an introductory level text, but this is already deeper than the knowledge that I commonly encounter on the gun range, and even in the gyms to some extent. Technique has to follow skill development, and it must be mastered before you move on to procedures or tactics. But this is an industry of cart before horse for photo ops. Don't be like everyone else. If you take this seriously, and you want to be an effective fighter, work the steps diligently. It will pay off.

PROCEDURES

Procedures come well after the basic skills are mastered and techniques have been developed to a reliable and repeatable level of performance. A procedure is a selected group of skills and techniques performed together to respond to a specific situation. How you combine those skills and techniques will depend on the circumstances of the problem you face. How you approach a doorway; how you deal with multiple attackers; every set of problems can be answered with a procedural response (or a series of procedures). It is very important to note that two things must be in place before you can begin training at a procedural level: highly developed skills, and the intuitive understanding of the fundamentals of fighting.

Highly Developed Skills and Techniques

The only road to procedural level training begins with bringing fundamental skills and techniques to a very highly developed, subconscious performance level. There are several reasons for this. First, you absolutely cannot stack skills and techniques together to be performed simultaneously, on demand, or in tandem without having them burned into your brain at a level that no longer requires conscious thought to perform them. It's just not possible to perform multiple skills together on demand if each one of those skills is not perfected and can be employed without much mental effort.

One of the places this becomes apparent is in CQB training. When students are tasked with learning procedures like a door procedure, they are not being asked to do things that they can't already do in isolated tasks: walk, take position, recognize the area of responsibility, open the door, enter the room. Each task, by itself, is pretty easy. However, when the student is asked to *make the decisions* of when to perform them simultaneously or consecutively, under pressure, while still evaluating and responding to the environment, that is when you watch shooters fall apart. The funny thing is, even the skills that they have developed to a decent level will quickly deteriorate when they have to put too much thought into other tasks that they have not developed in. You will see fast, great shooters who can *smoke show* the square range shoot like amateurs when they get put under procedural pressure.

This is why it is so important to only move as fast as you can process your environment and task list. It also shows that while you may be able to perform those skills without thinking on the range, you can't perform them while you're busy thinking about something else that is important. This is the important distinction that the square range cannot teach you.

So, it becomes very clear who has their fundamental skills like weapons manipulations, marksmanship, movement, etc. burned into their brain at a subconscious level, and who doesn't. It takes this level of challenge to finalize that process of truly owning a skill set. It must be prioritized out of the decision-making process, yet still be performed flawlessly with high accountability. This is also the moment to NOT loosen up on your standards. Do not be one of those people who think that opening up groups inside of a shoothouse or "pressure" situation is OK. It is not OK. You need to be able to maintain high standards throughout all levels of challenge to your skill sets. Maintain that 4-inch head and 8-inch chest preferred area. Everything outside of that is a failure, because a really bad guy will make you pay for a failure to neutralize, and that payment can be permanent.

Intuitive Principles in Procedures

Intuition is not a "sixth sense" telling you some esoteric information not discernible to the naked eye. Intuition is, quite simply, *the ability to immediately understand something without conscious reasoning.* This is where the details get deep. To understand the principles is a deeper understanding than just having a "why", as I have discussed previously. The principles of a task far outweigh the "why" of it because the "why" will be circumstantial, but the principles will apply across changing circumstances.

For example, if you employ a procedure to set up an area of denial with your muzzle down a hallway in your home, and you set up on the right side of the threshold on your end, the "why" could be because the other end feeds from the left so this cover provides the longest angle of coverage with the least amount of exposure to you. However, if you are ever faced with a threshold and hallway that you are not familiar with, you will need to quickly and intuitively recognize the problems and understand the principles and techniques that will solve those problems. Where are my angles of exposure and what position offers me the best coverage of them? What provides the most efficient positioning

102

without getting into other problems with furniture, doors, obstacles, etc.? So, you see that while it may be easy to master something in one environment with pre-planned strategies, it requires an intuitive application of the principles and the skills and techniques to apply them to a situation in an unfamiliar environment.

Operating at the procedural level is fighting. Plain and simple. When situations unfold you cannot rely on rehearsals and repetitions to get you through. You must have an immediate, intuitive understanding of the problems you face, the principles of the solutions, and the skills and techniques that need to be applied to those principles. We see this so often with CCW people in surveillance videos of robberies. They rely on the false sense of security that just having a gun gives them, and maybe the little bit of skill they exhibited on a square range. However, when they are approached by a savvy thug who closes distance on them before they can respond and proceeds to gain position on them before initiating the fight, they are like fish out of water.

At that point it becomes a procedural problem where recognition, positioning, angles, and timing all come into play on top of whatever skills will be needed to apply against those variables. Every person, professional or civilian, who carries a gun should train up to the procedural level. The problem is that it takes a long time of dedicated, monotonous work on the fundamental skills and mindset to be able to even begin training and testing at a procedural level. If you truly want to be an effective fighter, you have to put in the time, with proper guidance and feedback.

Procedures are collections of skills and techniques applied simultaneously or consecutively in response to a problem or series of problems. Fights are made up of problems. Often, that means many fast moving, changing variables and restrictive environments that will compound those problems. Have procedures for dealing with likely problems: multiple attackers, attacks while in your vehicle, home invasions at night, home invasions during the day, dealing with doors, hallways, rooms, and so on.

Attend training with instructors that specialize in each of these things. There are instructors who are known for working the close fight, others who are specialists at CQB (doors, hallways, rooms), and still others who are good in vehicle work. Seek them out and develop your own procedural level of tools in your tool box. But first, develop those fundamental skills and that intuitive level of recognition of the principles of fighting. It all starts and ends there. Conditioning leads to high level skill, proprioceptive awareness and technique development. When coupled with an intuitive understanding of the principles of fighting, procedural level training is within your grasp.

TACTICS

Do you even know what the word "tactical" means? That word is the absolute most abused word in the training world. I really try not to even use it. A good friend of mine, a very experienced instructor and SWAT guy, has a saying about this that always makes me laugh. He says, "you could write the word *tactical* on a bag of dogshit and some motherfucker somewhere would pay money for it." I am pretty sure he is right. In classes, I always ask students to define the word tactical. Very rarely can anyone correctly define it. Before you read any further, what is your definition of "tactical"?

Quite simply, the definition of tactic is: an action or strategy carefully planned to achieve a specific end. Most people, especially civilians, will never reach a truly "tactical" level of training. You'll notice in my taxonomy, "tactics" comes after skills, techniques and procedures. In my view, tactics actually have less application in *self-defense*, since it involves heavily pre-planned series of actions across a situation, rather than *responding* to said situation.

Think in terms of self-defense and rules of engagement. If what you did ended in the death of someone and you also admit to strategically planning that specific end, you could have quite a hard time in court. While there are some good reasons to pre-plan for events like home invasions and other scenarios that may happen in a predictable area, it must not be disregarded that you cannot pre-plan a death blossom ambush that would undeniably result in someone's death without expecting your plan to be scrutinized for your possible conviction. Like it or not, it is the society we live in.

Aside from that fun legal fact, tactics are a collection of skills, techniques and procedures applied to a specific set of problems to achieve a specific end *according to a predetermined plan.* In terms of training, it is way down the road from fundamentals work. For the civilian, it may apply to fighting around vehicles and home defense, for example. But I would argue staying within mission parameters, and being realistic, would require one to be more on the *procedural level,* allowing them to *respond* to each evolution in a fluid situation, rather than having a set plan that forces the situation actor to adhere to that plan regardless of changing circumstances. It is very important to understand that difference. Remember how I explained how objectives will change inside of a mission for the average person in a defense situation? Tactical planning tends to limit that ability to change and locks the plan to achieve specific objectives regardless of changes in circumstances.

Since this is an introductory level book, I am not going to go into any detail about *tactical* training here. If you are ever ready for tactical level training, or it is required for your job, the opportunities will be opened up for you. Until then, focus on fundamental skills and getting to a procedural level with your skills. In this text, the orientation work will take on a more tactical nature. The absolute and rampant misuse and abuse of the word "tactical" has misguided many people. But, it is the cool factor, so if it brings people in, great. Once they're in, let's all do our part to clarify the meaning of words. Meanings matter.

STANDARDS

Without standards--which are minimum acceptable skill levels measured in time, accuracy, capability, endurance, etc--you have no idea what your capabilities are or if your training is actually accomplishing anything beneficial. Standards can come in the form of shooting tests, timed drills, endurance and physical fitness stress, etc. Many tests exist such as the FBI qualifications, various police qualifications, military qualifications, and more. It is important to adopt or create minimum standards that fit into your mission and continually work to perform up to (and beyond) them.

Competition shooting can satisfy some of that but remember that there is a difference between the requirements of a competition and the demands of a fight. A *huge* difference. Keep that in mind when testing skill-based abilities through competition. Competition scores or classifications are not representations of overall capabilities used in a lethal force incident.

Another huge reason to have standards, especially if you are an agency or do business as a training company, is that standards (and well-written curriculum) are necessary when called to give deposition following a shooting or fight involving one of your agents, officers or students. Without standards, not only can you not stand behind your teaching and/or practices, but you have nothing but hearsay to go to court with if you are called out. And if a student or someone else is trying to save their own ass, they just might say anything, and it will be simply your word against theirs.

Professionalism is our goal

Heavily documented curriculum, standards and performance records are the practices of true professionals. When I am designing my courses, or teaching on the range, I am always working with one goal in mind: to teach people how to be professionals. There is no reason why someone carrying a gun should not be held to standards of professionalism, both in conduct and in capabilities. If you are going to carry a gun, you should be professional about it. This is mandatory if you choose to carry a gun for your job. This does not mean that you have to be a SWAT Jesus operator ninja. What it means is that *you should be able to meet a minimum requirement of safety and accuracy with your weapon and conduct yourself with self-control and discretion under pressure.*

The difference is in how we define "minimum". I personally do not accept the standards set forth by the NRA; literally anyone can become a certified instructor for them in one weekend. (While I support the organization in principle, they need to experience a changing of the guard for sure.) For my own program, you can't assist instruct with me until you've completed at least 50 hours of training as a student in my, or another approved, program and then helped as a range safety officer for 100 or more hours, and those requirements are not a guarantee of being selected. That only gets you to help with range safety. I also find many law enforcement qualifications to be severely substandard as well, requiring as few as 25 rounds hitting *anywhere* on the silhouette target from static positions to encompass an entire qualification to carry a weapon. We should hold ourselves to a higher standard. It is good to learn and pass the qualification course for your State or local law enforcement agency, especially for deposition purposes, but you should seek to create or adopt and modify other courses which require more stringent performance standards as well. Everything I do will both meet and surpass the requirements of recognized qualifications that I view as subpar. The training is designed to prepare you for the demands of the mission. The standards are the levels of performance we aspire to reach through our training, a way of having some level of confidence that we can actually perform some of the tasks that may be required.

The difference between "qualification" and "training"

Before we delve into standards, let's talk about the difference between "qualification" and "training". Do you believe that because someone has taken a concealed carry course they are now *proficient* in employing a weapon safely and effectively in a fast-moving deadly confrontation? Or that someone who has hunted and been a recreational shooter all of their life is thereby skillful enough to handle a weapon safely in a gunfight around innocent and panicking people? Do you believe that because a police officer has completed the academy and carries a gun every day in his or her job that he or she is an expert gun handler and shooter? If you answered "yes" to any of those questions, then you have mistaken "qualification" with mission-based standards of performance.

As a society, we are taught from a very young age to achieve nothing more than proficiency and qualification in order to get our reward. All through life, from grade school and into adulthood, it is memorization by rote that wins you grades, status, positions, salaries, authority, etc. Memorize some information, perform a mock-up of skills and pass a test; you are now "qualified" and "entitled" to a certain status/paycheck/privilege. As Paul Howe (U.S. Army Special Operations Ret.) puts it, "Minimums. We have become a society that strives for the minimum standard, and this is how we live our lives."

This method of doing things is so pervasive in our world that most of the public put all of their trust into these resultant qualifications. When we see someone, who is licensed or commissioned to do a particular job, we believe that they have been taught the ins and outs of that job and that they have at some point "proven their proficiency" in the job in order to have become officially qualified. Often, we not only trust that they are proficient and qualified, we believe they are *experts*. I mean, they are licensed or commissioned and have obviously been taught all of the aspects of that job, right?

Unfortunately, qualification by way of proficiency examinations does not make experts. In fact, it doesn't even weed out the inept. Life is fluid, demanding and unpredictable. It is a thinking person's world. Someone can be completely stellar at memorizing information and performing particular movements or operations in a testing environment, yet go on to completely fall apart under the pressure of a real-life situation. An officer or concealed carry civilian can be an excellent marksman on the range in front of a static target, yet not be able to hit anything when stress is induced, and the blood begins filling with the chemicals of fear. In fact, most are not excellent at any of it to begin with. It happens all of the time.

As a defensive firearms instructor, I am an instructor of deadly force. Of course, I teach gun safety, general awareness and avoidance. I instruct on ways to de-escalate and defuse a confrontation. But sometimes a situation has to go all the way and there is no safe avenue of escape; it has to be stopped with deadly force. Proper training must ultimately consider this as a final result. Whether it is a civilian looking for defensive concealed carry training, or a law enforcement officer looking to improve his or her skills, the end result is preparation for those worst-case, high-stress, rapidly changing and unpredictable confrontations.

The problem is that not one common qualification requirement that certifies someone to carry a gun in public ensures that the civilian, or officer, can actually operate the weapon safely or effectively during a high-stress, life or death, decision making encounter. Even though it is the very reason they will be carrying a gun--to prepare for that eventuality--*it simply is not required to be trained for that eventuality.* In many instances for law enforcement and civilians both, you only need to exhibit safe gun handling and minimal marksmanship under semi-pleasant, controlled conditions on static targets. Some states do not even require this for civilians.

For example, in Ohio where I used to offer CCW certification, civilians must complete an 8 hour course on gun safety and handling that consists of 6 hours of prescribed topics in the classroom and a minimum of 2 hours of live-fire range time. Anyone with a weekend NRA certification can teach it. There is no mandatory minimum of rounds that must be shot on target, and there is not an annual re-qualification. Even though the CCW license allows the civilian to carry a loaded gun in a holster in public, courses are not required to even cover holstering or un-holstering a loaded and chambered handgun safely. The class need only be completed safely, and, in most cases, you will be certified.

While there are no statistics available on how many rounds the average concealed carry citizen fires in practice yearly, we can make a safe bet that most of those rounds are fired under lax conditions, gun already out of the holster, at static targets. Sadly, most believe that because they have a ccw license, and because they are able to operate a gun well enough to hit a static target, they are done with training. Of course, I fully support the freedom to carry a weapon for self-defense, but I don't support the laziness of those who do not take it upon themselves to better train for it.

For police officers in most States, the State certification requires as low as a 25-round test, again shot at static targets. In fact, according to nationwide law enforcement estimates, an overwhelming majority of officers fire an average of less than 100 rounds per year in practice and qualification. Due to budget cuts in departments across the nation, training is the first thing to be cut. Qualification requirements have also consistently been reduced and shortened.

All too often qualification requirements and training needs are reduced due to budgetary concerns, lack of ammunition availability, lack of training facilities, etc. To quote an NYPD officer commenting anonymously on this topic to the New York Times following an investigation into a police involved shootings back in 2012:

"The department has "a factory line" approach to weapons training in which officers "get the basics — breathing, trigger control, but not much else. It's very brief, minimal. Firearms training is important — it's very important, and it's something that is not taken seriously," the officer concluded. (Alan Feurer, Ready, Aim, Ready?, New York Times Dec.8 2012)

Given the very low frequency that officers train/practice and the low standards of qualifications, is there any wonder why, when the FBI police-involved shooting statistics are released, they indicate officers' accuracy nationwide is 15%-20%. That means statistically about 80% of officer-fired rounds in deadly confrontations are complete misses. Many of those rounds end up injuring innocent bystanders and hostages. It's a safe bet that many officers themselves were injured due to them failing to stop a threat in time because they could not hit the suspect(s) with effective fire.

Now, this is not an indictment of the process of qualification nor is it an attack on those who do not train harder, per se. While I do personally believe that firearm qualification requirements for both police and civilians are extremely low, the problem we face has more to do with *our perspective on being qualified versus actually being prepared* to operate a gun in a high stress event. What we need to do is push the educational aspect of gun fighting to the point where people understand that being able to put a predetermined number of holes in a target from a prescribed distance in a controlled environment in no way, shape or form prepares you for a deadly confrontation. Nor does it give you ANY idea how you will perform or shoot in said confrontation.

There are many levels to the knowledge of fighting. Fighting with a gun is no different, it is still fighting. It is, in fact, a martial art. Stance, grip, motions of the draw, balance, leverage, explosive movement, fast reaction times—all of these apply in gun fighting as much as they do in hand-to-hand combat. *You do not walk into a martial arts dojo, spend 8 or 20 hours with an instructor and walk out an expert with a high-ranking belt. Nor would strapping on that belt every day for five or ten or twenty years magically make you a fighting expert. Yet, that is exactly how many feel about the gun.* After a qualification course for a firearm, while you may walk out with a gun license or commission, you are not an expert. Nor are you prepared to deal with a deadly confrontation based upon that certification alone. Solid shooting instruction that focuses on the fundamentals and the mechanics of the shot is a good place to start. But when you take solid shooting instruction and mix it with induced-stress drills, force-on-force testing and a good dose of mindset training, you end up with a winning combination that can produce an acceptable level of performance.

The fighter with the most longevity is not the most intelligent, strongest or biggest. It's the one who adapts to change the most successfully. You can be the greatest static marksman on the range. You can be the strongest and fastest shooter, on the range. But when a real life or death situation happens, environment and circumstances are very rarely ideal in the sense that you would have plenty of time to get your stance just right, line your sights up, take your time deciding what to do, etc.

Most gunfights are over in a matter of seconds and usually happen in extremely close quarters and less than ideal environmental conditions. The only thing that will prepare you to adapt your decision making and skills to those rapidly changing factors is realistic, defensive training that encompasses fundamental skills, high-speed decision making, force-on-force testing, and self-control mindset. That training should push you to an established standard level of performance in all tasks. Don't let your standards be a subpar qualification course, set the bar high and work toward that level consistently. Most importantly, don't fool yourself into believing that a simple qualification course means you are ready for battle.

Experience Driven Lessons

Many years ago, there was a school shooting near me in Ohio. The first responding officer encountered the shooter in the school and fired one round, that missed. The shooter escaped through a door and went on to shoot a few more people. That same officer encountered the shooter again and fired 14 rounds, only hitting him 3 times and none of those in critical zones, which was representative of an average performance in a shooting based on nation-wide numbers. In no way am I debasing that officer on a personal level. However, when we look at history we need to look at the "improves" and not just the "sustains." We talk an awful lot about "heroes" and not enough about how we could have been faster, safer and more effective. Fuck your feelings; we need to talk about this.

The truth is that we are doing better as a nation with our performance, but not on a wide enough scale. My desire is for gun carrying civilians to begin to see this as a problem for themselves and to work to correct it, just like *some* of the professionals in law enforcement have been actively doing. You are very likely not as ready as you think you are. Believe me, I make it my job to deconstruct false confidence and to cause untested plans to fail for people. I have watched it happen so many times that I know, most are not ready.

In a recent shooting during the writing of this book, one of the worst our nation has seen, a disturbed, criminally violent person walked into a church with an AR15 and killed at least 26 people. Men, women, children, infants...all dead. During the shooting, a neighbor was alerted to a figure dressed in tactical gear firing into the church across the street. He rushed to his safe, opened it and grabbed his rifle and a handful of rounds, and began loading a mag on his way out the door. In the meantime, a killer was walking up and down the aisle and executing anyone still breathing between the pews, men, women, children, and taking his time doing it. As the killer was leaving the church he was engaged by the neighbor with an AR15. The killer was wounded in the firefight and subsequently died after a high-speed car chase.

I want to say that the man is a hero if, for nothing else, *going to the sound of guns*. It takes a special type of man to run toward gunfire with the mission of saving lives. He should be forever commended for that. If you are near an active shooter that is clearly slaughtering people and you are "called" to fight, by all means, you take that fight right to the devil. But just like the cop in the school shooting I cited above, what can we look at to determine how we could have been faster, safer and more effective? Having magazines loaded and ready? I mean, if you have a rifle, and it's in a safe, what would it hurt to have some mags ready to go? How about fundamental skill effectiveness under stress? A 25-yard gunfight with an AR15 should yield very high accuracy results.

Sometimes, when you are preparing, or struggling with fundamentals under stress, people are dying. And any prolonging of the incident, including high speed chases and standoffs, present the opportunity for more people to die. How prepared and capable we are is measured in our performance to our standards. If you don't have standards, then you are not prepared. I judge these situations harshly because they piss me off. And they should piss you off. Hopefully to the point that you get off of your ass and seek a performance level that will actually save lives in a faster, safer and more effective way. When the bad wolf starts attacking, the faster and more capable wolf puts him down. Quickly and decisively. Performance matters.

We need to get away from the attitude that you can't say anything that's perceived "negative" about someone who did a good thing. We also need to stop using the excuse that "you never know how you'll respond, so they did the best they could. It would probably happen to you, too!" We are capable of post-event analysis, of learning, and of improving our performance based on those lessons learned. But first we have to let ourselves learn them.

Training has become a legitimate subculture, and that is amazing. 10 years ago, a civilian couldn't find any place to train in gun fighting or tactics, and back then law enforcement was seriously constricted to the institutional inbreeding of training within their own agencies. Today, you can literally find *kick ass* training every single week in most regions of the country. It is quite literally everywhere, and not just for civilians but for law enforcement as well. So many guys are out there with 15 to 30 years on busy SWAT teams and task forces, or 10 to 20 years of combat and special operations experience from the GWOT, now offering their experience to good people to help make them better. Training the fighting man is a full-blown industry. We've even moved past the range ninja phase and have matured as an industry and a community to the point where we are focusing on practical skills, techniques, procedures and tactics.

Developing standards

For myself and my students, I score basic qualification targets based on an 8" circle body zone and a 3" x 5" head zone. Some qualifications I move to a 6" and even down to a 4" body circle. None of them are very clearly outlined in a way that is visible past 10 yards or so on a clear day, which means that you have to develop the ability to group shots in a given area without a visual aid target. For my scoring, anything outside of those areas is a miss plain and simple. There are no "B" or "C" zones. I did not come to this conclusion right away in my training career. It took a few years of trial and error and then some exposure to true professionals. Watching leaders hold shooters to high standards within a fighting context showed me that it was both possible and necessary. The alternative is just unacceptable.

Who you are and what your life is like is a direct result of your standards. Most people are content to perform the minimum. The minimum effort, time, and ambition to get the paycheck and get home. The problem with that here is that we are now dealing with a life and death consequence. When guns come out, lives are on the line. People can and often will die. Why would you be content with not knowing that you can at least put rounds into a precise area with speed and efficiency? Why would you not want to know to the best of your ability that you have trained the fundamentals until they will not clog up your thinking in the heat of the moment because you do not need to think about weapon manipulation and shot placement, you just know how to do it? Developing standards of accuracy and time will help to know these important skills are in order. Here are some guidelines you can follow to create standards that will help ensure that your confidence is real, and your skills are truly reliable:

- Create an all or nothing standard for shooting, where you are in the 8, 6 or 4-inch zone or you have missed, nothing outside of the lines counts. In fact, quit accepting hits that touch the line. Stop accepting mediocrity and poor performance as being "good enough". Inside the hit zone or it's a miss, plain and simple. Delete "B" and "C" zones forever.
- Create a distance measure for that accuracy performance. When you can stay inside of the prescribed hit zones at a given distance, move to the next 3 to 5 yards back and start again.
- Make sure that distances get close enough to ensure mechanical offset is accounted for, and far enough away to make sure that optic use transitions back to being closer to point of aim/point of impact, all within one qualification.
- Create a time component for the deployment of your weapon with the accuracy standard being met. For example, if you carry a concealed pistol, set a standard time you need to be able to draw the handgun from concealment and fire accurate shots into the preferred area. Then work to meet that standard at increasing distances. Reduce the time requirement as the target gets closer. The same goes if you carry in a duty holster, or you want to work on rifle deployment. Start with the weapon where it would usually be and work from there.
- Examine the mission you have and determine what the likely demands will be. Make your standards realistic for the demands of your mission.
- Determine right from the start what is "passing" and what is not. For me, and other professionals that I trust, the standard is 100%, passing is 80%. Any complete missing of the silhouette is a fail for the qualification.
- Create a "quick qualification" that measures the performance to these standards that can easily be completed in 20 minutes or so at the beginning and end of a training day. This can be as short as very demanding 30

116

rounds in courses of fire from 3 yards to 25 yards. It can also serve as a good lunch break shooting session. In other words, it needs to be something that can be completed without a major production or time requirement. I stole this "quick qual" idea from Joe Weyer, SWAT Commander and Training Officer for the Alliance, Ohio team, because it's an awesome way to keep people honest and make sure it gets done regularly. Alliance is one of the few departments that I have seen who will actually bench or even suspend officers for failing the department's own qualification, and I fully support that practice. If you can't take that part of your job seriously enough to meet a minimum standard, perhaps it isn't the job for you.

- Create a more thorough qualification that can be done periodically to more thoroughly test skills. I personally use a version of the "Hackathorn Standards" that I adopted and modified for my own interpretation of what my mission demands will be. This should be a multiple target, multiple position, multiple distance qualification that involves the use of cover and some movement over a 60-round course of fire. The accuracy standard is maintained at the "hit or miss" level, no exceptions.

You must set a standard that leaves that 100% typically just out of your reach to use it as a qualification, but not so hard that no one (including you) can pass it. What good is a qualification that no one can pass? I have seen instructors take students through a qualification that even that instructor could not pass. Everybody has bad days, but be careful about this. To consistently do that is just counterproductive and quite frankly does nothing for bringing value to the students. The trouble is how do we go about creating a standard that is demanding but realistically achievable? You can begin with any of the multitude of standards and qualifications that already exist, such as the FBI qualification, and work from there to modify it to your mission. I strongly suggest implementing tougher accuracy standards ("hit or miss" as outlined above) as the first modification of whatever you borrow from other quals.

The same approach can be used to set physical fitness standards as well. If you want to adopt a standard from someone else, take a close look at the average person who passes that standard and determine if you want to be better than them. In most cases, you should want to have a higher standard than what is approved by a department or agency. If the average person who passes that qual is by your standards out of shape, then maybe that's a clue that you should modify it to higher demands.

In the end, the important factor here is that we are seeking a level of performance goals that are deemed professional by having elements of reliability, advanced safety, effectiveness and efficiency. Simply stop accepting mediocrity and "good enough".

CHAPTER SEVEN: TESTING AND VALIDATION

PERCEPTION VS REALITY

There are three categories of knowledge about fighting skill-sets:

1. Hypothesis: a supposition or proposed explanation made on the basis of limited evidence as a starting point for further investigation. An assumption of ability without ANY evidence that it is actually an ability.
2. Theory: a coherent group of substantiated factors, commonly regarded as correct, that can be used as principles of explanation and prediction for a class of phenomena. An assumption based upon testing and verification.
3. Fact of Experience (Real Life): Retrospective. It happened, how did you perform?

Like far too many CCW citizens, police and security officers out there carrying guns today, many people are walking around with completely untested and unproven hypotheses about their own abilities. Without ever going on to a range more than once or twice (if that) and actually practicing getting the gun out of the holster quickly, they have convinced themselves that they can not only do it, but can do it under serious stress of danger and time constraints. It's just ridiculous to walk around with assumptions about your abilities when you have not repeatedly performed these assumed abilities at all. But people do it. Everyday.

Testing in fight training is critically important for the confidence part of your orientation (a topic we are moving closer to). It is also absolutely the only way you can know how you will perform without actually getting into a real, deadly fight. Without being able to repeatedly get into real fights, which no reasonable person wants to do, you can only *test* your skills and techniques in varied ways to develop a level of substantiated confidence that you can repeatedly perform them on demand.

However you do it, you have to work away from the untested hypothesis and into a tested theory. Set a simple task and test it. Can I get my gun out and hit a target at 7 yards in under 2 seconds? If I stand on the range and perform that a few hundred times, I can answer that question affirmatively and confidently that I am at least *capable* of doing it. Conditioning myself to do it under threat is another task, but at least the confidence of knowing I can do it at all is unquestionable. Do you get the point? This will greatly reduce the chance of uncertainty causing me to hesitate or second guess myself when that white-hot moment arises and it's time to act for real. We often say, you don't know what you don't know. Testing and Real Life are the only two ways to find out what you really know, and what you don't know. Which one would you rather be surprised at, testing or real life and death danger?

The importance of sparring and force-on-force

The best way to accomplish the validation of your tactics, techniques and procedures (TTP's) is in Force on Force (FoF) training. For combatives (hand-to-hand fighting) that means sparring and grappling. For firearms training, that means some type of simulated training ammunition (or at a minimum gas airsoft). Get into real fights with real people, using weapons that actually sting you, preferably firing high quality simulated ammunition from real firearms converted to fire the special cartridges, and in courses designed and guided by experienced gunfighters who know how to design training objectives. There, you can test all of your hypotheses out. Can you draw on someone who already has a gun out on you and win? Can you negotiate corners in a house and not expose yourself? Can you make quick decisions under pressure? So many questions can be answered with a lot of undeniable clarity in an FoF course. This is why it is called "validation". You are validating the information you've gathered and the skills that you have practiced.

It is literally mindless to walk around with equipment and plans that you have not tested. Why would anyone reasonably make the decision to do so? Only in a society where your overall likelihood of being attacked is so low that most people skate by without encountering real violence can you make such decisions and defend them. And that is OK, if that is how you want to play the odds. The difference is between knowing and guessing; just be sure to make that distinction when your plan includes tactics, techniques or procedures that you have never tested. No training plan is complete without the testing and validation component. Unless you can prove that a) you are capable of executing the plan under pressure and b) the plan actually works under pressure, you simply have no idea that what you are spending your time and money learning will actually apply to saving yours or someone else's life.

Do you think it would be a great idea to have a boxer only ever practice on a bag, and then throw him into a full match against a trained opponent in the ring? What about taking someone and showing them jiu jitsu moves in drill form for slow practice, and then putting them into a competition against experienced opponents? Neither would be a good idea, just like shooting at paper targets a few times wouldn't prepare you to fight against a violent, and most likely more experienced, opponent. In boxing or jiu jitsu sparring is the method of validation before a match or competition is ever entered. In gun fighting, it's simulated ammunition training in force-on-force. Some call this *pressure testing*. It's where you actually test the skills and procedures you have learned to see if they can actually work against a real attacking opponent.

HOW TO SET UP VALIDATION

There is a clear difference between quality FoF validation and run of the mill paintball or airsoft. The same goes for rolling on the mat. While it can be fun to get out and go all-out in a battle with those tools, without the guidance of an experienced instructor there will be no real learning objectives with clear paths to achieve them. Aimlessly running around and gunning, or rolling on the mat night after night, will not ultimately validate much in the way of real defensive plans. In fact, truly good FoF training will be relatively low on round count. I have a few observations for validation, both from running it and from being a student of it.

It must be realistic

When I teach a force on force class, I personally set up scenarios of the type a civilian may face, such as walking into a robbery in a gas station, or being approached by surprise after a night out on your way from the car to the door of your house. These are based upon very likely events that have happened and continue to happen every day. It also puts the defender in the very real position of disadvantage, since most criminals will strike by ambush or at least take the high ground for control. More importantly, it teaches the student that simply having a gun is not enough to solve a problem. You must be able to assess, think, plan, and employ procedures to solve complicated problems. I don't care how good you are, not one person is capable of watching 360 degrees around them 100% of the time. When you are caught slipping, you will need a lot more than a gun in your holster to fix it. Training like this teaches those other skills.

It must have clear learning objectives

It doesn't do anyone a service to have scenarios or "fights" that simply test skills. You can test skills with standards in that manner. There must be a learning objective to every run or scenario in an FoF course. Learning objectives can be things like learning how to maneuver safely around no-shoots while under pressure or engaging a fight. It can be problem solving on a mental level, or developing strategy through assessment and recognition of opportunity. There may be other elements like the use of white light in low-light situations, etc. Whatever the case, the program should be designed based on experience and be realistic to the mission of the student for the purpose of learning something very specific from the run.

For combatives, simply wrestling over a gun or taking on multiple attackers isn't enough to qualify as a learning objective. There should be other elements involved for specific application of skills to be tested. As an example, I like to start a weapon retention exercise after the shots are fired and at the point where the gun is grabbed, and the attacker also has a knife or blunt weapon (because I refrain from teaching people to shoot unarmed attackers outside of narrow extenuating circumstances). This creates the need to apply all of the combatives skills like base, control, joint manipulation, and weapon retention while dealing with a non-compliant attacker for a specific objective: weapon retention and control simultaneously.

Don't practice dying

The student should never be taught to die. Make them fight through, always and every time. This embeds in them a will to fight, and reinforces that you are not out of the fight until the lights go out. Attackers should be ordered to drop after a set number of hits, but the student defender should be ordered to fight all the way through. After a run, you can count hits the student took and use it as a teaching point of, "you may likely die from that and we need to do better" but you never tell them to lay down in a fight. I stabbed someone 23 times before he went down. I have been sliced and stabbed and never went down in those fights. I watched someone get stabbed 56 times and he never went down. I even witnessed a guy take a .357 Magnum right in the ass above his right leg and not only did he not go down, he ran 6 blocks with the speed and stride of an athlete. Any good FoF training will unconsciously and consciously embed the will to fight through in every student that can handle it.

123

Safety procedures change

Force on force, especially with simulated ammunition, is not a purely safe endeavor. If you are using UTM or Simunition, it is very possible to get penetrated by a round, especially in soft areas like the neck, face, head, eyes, etc. Greater safety precautions must be in place and strictly enforced. One rule that I like is the "no visible skin exposed rule." This eliminates the exposure of soft points to the ammunition. There are several other precautions that should be added to your typical firearms safety rules. Another rule that I think is very important is the sterilization of the training area from all other weapons and ammunition. Knives, asp's, OC spray, magazines, etc. are all removed completely from the staging and training areas to prevent any contamination of dangerous weapons into a fighting environment. Too many mistakes can be made, and when adrenaline is high, mistakes become more common. Full protection of face, head, neck and vitals should still be in place at all times. Put in place a very stringent safety plan for FoF and stick to it like the gestapo. And if you attend a course that does not do this, remember it is your own health and well-being on the line.

TRAINING WITHOUT VALIDATION IS JUST GUESSING AT BEST

Everything you train needs to go through a validation process of testing. The only way to safely do that without getting into real fights is through force on force and sparring. All training cycles should conclude to validation, and then subsequently continue or start a new cycle. This is why it is important to maintain standards and perform to them. The standards are ways to maintain the skills without the rigors and costs of continuous testing. It should be noted that too much focus on lack of experience can cause doubt. Uncertainty is the greatest enemy of all fighters, and it simply occupies empty space in your mind when faced with the fight. Force on force validation is a way to fill that empty space before that day comes. Replace uncertainty with certainty by repeatedly performing to standards, and sometimes passing validation against non-compliant opponents with the skills you have trained.

One of the overlooked (or unknown) benefits of FoF validation is a greater ability to enjoy life. This is one of the things that I push hard in my coursework. Validation gives you the most valuable advantage in the fight: true confidence. True confidence also allows you to relax when there is not a fight, like when you are out with family in public and enjoying some activity. My background is quite different, but I am able to now enjoy my life and my company, even when in public, because I know with certainty that I am myself a dangerous predator, and I am even more aware when I am relaxed and not caught up in a "scanning tunnel vision" mode. The skills, techniques, procedures and tactics are on a switch. They've been thoroughly tested and validated, and I am confident in my skills and decision making no matter when they are needed.

FoF validation is a chance to get those internal conversations heading in that direction. Without it, you really are just guessing and, while you can fool yourself in daily life, you won't buy into your own bullshit when your life is really on the line. Validate, and then you can have true confidence. Again, validation is the only way the unexperienced can gain true confidence.

CHAPTER EIGHT: OTHER TRAINING CONSIDERATIONS

SPORT TRAINING VS FIGHT TRAINING

One thing that requires attention as an instructor is making sure you are teaching always within your lane. Even when you are experienced, it is not an easy thing to always do. It's very easy to grab "cool" stuff to teach that doesn't necessarily apply to your student's likely outcomes or come from your particular experience. I work very hard to shave away anything that does not fall into the category of likely circumstances in a sudden civilian encounter with extreme violence. It's a good thing in that it allows for more time to spend on the things that most people need, which are the repeated fundamental skills, techniques and decision-making. It's not as great when it comes to marketing, but I never have sacrificed my principles for marketing.

Often times, I honestly have a hard time finding other instructors or even students who take classes professionally that can have a productive discussion about training for *fighting*. And therein lies the problem: not very many people understand truly violent fighting. It's a surprisingly complex subject with so many different avenues of experience available that even if you are experienced with one type of fighting, you can have little idea how to handle some other type that is out there. This is where that whole "stay in your lane" thing becomes so important.

For civilians, two overarching categories of fighting are *sport fighting*, and *criminal violence*. In sport fighting, you have traditional martial arts, MMA, boxing, and also some shooting competitions are held in this category (IDPA, USPSA). For criminal violence...well, what is it? Can you define the "style" of criminal violence? Most people can't define it in terms of what style of fighting it is. Or how to train for it. Sure, everyone wants to step up and tell us how their particular fighting style would be the best in a criminal violence encounter. But if all you have ever done is fight in the dojo, ring or cage, and even the few school yard and "bar fights" you've had, then you don't know that this system works the way you think it does. It's an untested hypothesis.

If "fighters" lack the experience of violence that it takes to know violence, then CCW citizens and most instructors are at an even greater deficit of knowledge. The chances of getting into a shooting are phenomenally lower than getting into a fist fight. The chances of getting into a gunfight for the average CHL citizen are extraordinarily slim to none. The chances of a law enforcement officer having a shooting in his or her career are also surprisingly low.

Here's what people do not think about. There are subsections of our society where the chances of all of it happening are not only very high, it's an everyday event. In 2016, Chicago had, by some estimates, 3361 shooting victims. 3361/365= about 9 people shot, on average, PER DAY. In one city. Given my experience, I'd say your chances of running into a subject matter expert on criminal violence fighting and gun fighting in Chicago are pretty damn good both in the professional law enforcement and in the criminal communities. In the early 80's to mid-90's, Youngstown/Warren/Cleveland were hellish. I remember, I was there. The neighborhood I lived in in Los Angeles was Hispanic gang territory; my street was the worst crime rate street in the Valley when I was there. And trust me, the shit those people do out there is way off the charts of what you would imagine, probably much like Chicago. My uncle Kenny was murdered in LA. He was severely beaten on his couch at home (as evidenced by the bloody scene left behind), and then taken to an orchard, dragged with a vehicle for about 500 feet and then shot 3 times in the head execution style. He was still alive when they found him, but died shortly after. Of course, he was a member of the world's largest 1% gang, so you live by the sword…

The point is that there are criminals out there who are seasoned in gunfights and murderous level violence. There are also good people who have grown up in those environments, did what they had to do to survive and somehow later made it out. Both of them know things about civilian criminal violence, and how to operate within it, that the "experts" can never know. There are guys in prisons right now that have upwards of 20 to 30 kills, and most of those against other combatants, not just weak victims. Why is this important? Because what your instructor is teaching you for self-defense *should* be to prepare you to meet these people. And if your instructor is not one of these people, or has not dealt with them extensively, then how does anyone know if what they are teaching/learning will be applicable?

If I had to identify one major problem in the civilian self-defense firearms training community, it would be the contamination of competition style shooting masquerading as "fight training" in self-defense firearms training. (There's also the problems of military/law enforcement team-based, supply chain supported training with their respective differences in rules of engagement and priority of life, being used in civilian training. But I would call competition contamination the overarching problem because I see it in those verticals as well.)

The problem is so bad, that whenever I talk to a "highly-trained" civilian about training, the conversation quickly devolves into "you have to shoot competition if you really want to get good." This is where it gets difficult to understand, so pay attention. While it is true that the best "shooters" on the planet are competition shooters, it is not even remotely true that they are the best fighters. So there is a disconnect in the definition of "fight training" at the root of the conversation. Are we talking about training for fighting, or training just for the shooting component? And if we are talking about training for the shooting component, then are we aware of, and capable of, separating the two topics and differentiating between the two very different mindsets and procedures needed for each?

Experience tells me that most people are not. It is because they truly do not understand fighting. In real lethal force encounters, you learn rather quickly that in the large scope of things, the weapon component is truly secondary in your considerations. What the experienced gang-banger or seriously violent criminal will have as an advantage over you is also the primary consideration of the fight process: decision making. Being able to shoot super fucking fast does not equate to making the difficult decisions that carry dire consequences, and making them with lightning speed while dealing with oncoming changing variables that will fuck your mind over tenfold. It just does not equate. The experienced criminal can do it. He's good at it. He has experience with it. He's a predator; he knows how to read you, your cues, your fear. His threat assessment model is highly developed, and his orientation to committing violence is superior because, culturally, he doesn't have any prohibitions like you do. If he is particularly dangerous, that is a testament to his skills and survivability, since being a violent criminal is somewhat of a dangerous profession with a high-mortality rate.

Fighting well requires three basic developments:
- A well-developed set of fundamental skills, techniques and procedures.
- The conditioning to physically perform them repeatedly.
- The mindset to make the correct decisions and push through adversity to be able to utilize those skills.

Competition is NOT deadly force stress inoculation. If I had ten bucks for every time someone has said "competition is the best training for gun fighting" in my presence, I'd be too busy spending my money to write this book. In all the times I have heard it, I can't recall it ever coming from someone who has been in real deadly confrontations. I'm not saying that experienced fighters won't recommend competition, they often do. But with most people we're back to that whole "lane" thing again, making comparisons between things you know and things you have no fucking idea about.

Competition may cause you stress, it is true. And I am certainly not going to be the asshole that repeats the cliche' "that'll get you killed in da streetz!" But I will say two things about that stress: *that it does not produce stress anywhere near a real fight (not even close)*, and; *it only produces that stress if you actually give a shit about the results and/or what people think of you.* In other words, if you don't care about the results and/or what other shooters will think of you, then there's literally nothing to get stressed about.

If you walk into a competition with no care about the results and no care about what others think, the precursor reasons that create the stress begin to diminish greatly. This is where competition *can* be useful. **If you can compete without allowing it to stress you out, I will argue that you are more correctly using it for deadly force training.** Of course, many will now say, "well, that's what we mean!" No, it isn't. You are trying to pedal the story that the stress of competition is a chance to perform your skills under "stress." What I am saying is that your goal should always be to control and minimize stress. It IS in your control, since stress is based solely upon your own perception. So, why not practice being able to compete in a non-life-threatening match without getting stressed out over something so terribly petty in comparison to someone trying to kill you?

Just like when we attend week-long shoothouse training, which can be a most stressful training situation (depending on who's teaching it), my goal is always to move through all of the training, performing at my highest level, without allowing my heart rate to move much above resting heart rate. THAT is why we are there, to achieve adaptive performance while experiencing minimal or diminishing stress. Don't confuse the two: seeking out stress for the purpose of performing jacked up vs. conditioning self-control for the purpose of adaptive performance at your highest level.

So as a student of fighting, think deeply about what it means to "stay in your lane" during training. Master that first. Analyze what someone teaches in this light. Training to fight is not only learning and practicing skills, it is largely learning how to think. Think of a violent attack as a complex riddle that must be solved in sudden layers, the success of each layer determines whether you get to go forward or not; and your book's ending is based off of the choices you had to make in nanoseconds. You could die or go to prison if you choose wrong.

Each quick decision you make has very real life-and-death, legal, and psychological consequences. What do you base your decisions on? What is your orientation to extreme violence? What process do you use for threat assessment? Clarify your foundation Mission statement. Develop a Training Protocol based on the likely requirements of your mission. If you deviate from that training protocol and compete, or take team-based training, ensure that you are not doing it under the illusion that you are training for your Mission's fight in particular, but rather you are looking for the universal underlying principles that will apply also to your mission.

As civilians, we focus on the unexpected occurrence of extreme civilian criminal violent attack while alone or with your family. There are layers of problems within that blanket scenario and more than enough to keep you focused throughout all of your training efforts.

THE LOST ART OF "WOODSHEDDING"

"Woodshedding" is a term that originated among musicians depicting the act of going into a woodshed or other isolated place to practice where no one could hear them. The mystique of it is that the artist would emerge one day with "sudden" new skills and dazzle onlookers with an unseen transformation. This isolated practice can be applied to any skill set, and it should be. The problem that we see today is primarily created by social media and the need to always be seen as something special.

Social media has conditioned us to believe that we have to perform constantly, and when you have grown up under the self-imposed microscope of social media, there likely is never a moment one feels safe to disengage and go to master a skill in privacy. This is unfortunate because something magical can happen when one goes to be alone with the process of mastery. And this doesn't necessarily mean "alone" today as much as it means away from the need to perform for a social audience all the time. The magic that takes place when we remove the influence of the audience is that we are allowed to make lots of mistakes without consequence, and to perfect before we perform.

I have achieved great heights in many different verticals by woodshedding. During that time, I will shy away from posting about it in social media, and will focus on learning, taking courses, practicing, working with mentors, etc. When the moment of competency or mastery comes, you now have a choice whether you want to share it with the world or keep it to yourself in the name of concealment and advantage. Without the woodshed, you have no choice. You will be judged and influenced, and mostly by people who have no real idea what they are talking about. Their influence is not only unnecessary; it can be damaging. If you have experienced a life-altering event, a divorce, death of a loved one, a serious injury, etc., you can benefit greatly from disengaging from the performance on the world's stage and remove that pressure from your learning process. You can relax, examine yourself, and determine if you really do want to do it. How many times have you started on a journey only to find out it isn't what you thought? Now how many times did you publicize that journey so much that you either felt ashamed to drop it, or worse you continued it because you publicly committed to it and kept doing it out of social pressure?

Woodshedding is a mandatory function of becoming a teacher. When you decide to teach a skill set, you should have the humility to know that you are not ready to tell the world you are a teacher the first day you decide to do it. This is something we see way too much of in the firearms community. When I decided to incorporate gun fighting into my instruction catalogue, I refrained from mass social media exposure and kept my work very local and largely unpublicized. Only after I had accumulated several thousand hours of range time, and had helped hundreds of people successfully, did I begin to call myself a gun fighting instructor publicly. And remember, I have experience with violent guncraft and weapons based violence. I had also been an instructor in combatives and fighting oriented fitness for about 10 years prior to teaching gun fighting. Even still, I believed it to be both humble and vital for my progress to woodshed before I presented myself on a larger stage.

Woodshedding allows you to bulletproof yourself for presentation to the unkempt masses. They will attack, and when they do, you will know both yourself and your craft well enough to weather that storm and stand firm on your positions. You will also develop the self-awareness to be a good student and have the humility to admit when presented with viable options you hadn't thought of, since you took the opportunity to seek out instruction and learn during that time as well. This very book is both the result of the process of woodshedding, and the culmination of many reinventions of myself through several woodshedding sessions throughout my life. When life throws new demands at you, or hits you so hard that everything you thought you knew has been shaken and cracked, you can always trust the woodshed to build something new. Sometimes, that time with ourselves is much more important to our growth than the actual skill we are working on.

Turn off the selfie machine and get to work.

TIPS ON CHOOSING INSTRUCTORS AND SCHOOLS

As I've said before, the self-defense industry and its subsequent categories of martial arts and gun fighting are full of "experts" who have never done the thing they are experts in. The problem is created and compounded by the fact that students themselves cannot know what they do not know yet. The lack of the instructor's experience creates gaps in the information that is taught. These gaps are not always apparent, and the student ends up walking away with incomplete information that they do not know is incomplete. Often, that instructor started out as one of those students and still is not aware that his information has a huge gap in it. As the student, you will actually believe you received thorough, reliable information that has prepared you for serious situations. You believe this because you had no prior frame of reference by which to judge that information; you simply are not experienced.

My focus in this book is on self-defense. Therefore, I am speaking about instructors who claim to be teaching "self-defense." This applies to not only firearms instructors but instructors in any type of martial training system, from jiu jitsu to gun fighting. One of the first litmus tests for a self-defense instructor is how they cover the rules, parameters and consequences of violence.

In order to be an effective, safe and thorough self-defense instructor, those rules, parameters and consequences should be woven into the very fabric of the system they teach. They should be central considerations in every drill and concept, those considerations are *that* important. Too often, instructors focus on the *fighting* part of the fight which, when applied without consideration to the rules and limitations of violence, can end in tragedy like a long prison sentence.

Another important characteristic of a good teacher is that they will be avid students themselves. Often times this is the only correction of the problem of incomplete information, that is, to learn what experience teaches *by proxy*. When you spend time under the tutelage of someone who has been there and done that, who is grounded in the realities of what real violence does to your life, you can begin to get a strong sense of what is important and what is not.

A good instructor will lower their ego and seek the teachings of those who have different experience than he or she does. I have been in a lot of real violence, yet even with more experience than most I regularly attend classes as a student under teachers that have *different* experiences than I do. I also have several instructors that attend my courses regularly as well. It is how it should be done.

So, who is the most qualified person to learn firearms and self-defense from? Law Enforcement? Ex-military? Navy Seals? Top Competition Shooters? Some of what I'm going to say here might not be popular with some people. This is all based on my opinion, so you can take it or leave it.. But that opinion is backed by a lot of real violence experience and thousands upon thousands of hours as both an instructor and student.

Police and Military: Public Illusion

First, I'm going to address the *public illusion* when it comes to firearms/self-defense instructors. There is a *blind respect* given to entire groups of people and/or occupations when it comes to firearms knowledge and the understanding of violence. As an instructor--and especially after some years working as a gun salesman--I cannot count the times that I have heard something along the lines of, "Find someone in law enforcement or military to teach you how to shoot, *they* know what they're doing."

So, let's define blind respect for our purposes: *full respect and acknowledgement given to someone for skills or knowledge despite never seeing any real evidence of said skills or knowledge.* It often sounds like this: "*Oh, your uncle is a cop? He must be a gun expert!*" Or, "*Your dad was in the military? I bet he really knows how to shoot!*" Or my favorite, "My dad was a marine. He taught me how to shoot so I don't need any training." This perception that everyone who's been in the military or law enforcement is automatically a firearms expert is just factually untrue. (Not to mention the deductive fallacy that military or law enforcement are ever trained in the ins and outs of civilian self-defense. They are not.)

If you have not seen hard evidence that a particular individual knows what they are doing, can handle a weapon safely and can shoot extremely well (as should be the case if they are going to instruct others), then you cannot truthfully say that this person is any sort of an expert at anything. You are assuming someone is an expert based solely on credentials or occupation. You are committing your first training error following the public illusion that an entire category of individuals are imbued with magical knowledge and skill by virtue of having an occupation that involves *some* gun training will be.

Let me tell you something, half of my family were military, including my dad and his father before him, and they are the LAST people on earth I would want to handle a gun next to me. I've watched my honorably discharged ex-military family members put at least a few rounds through the ceiling of the house I grew up in. And anyone who has spent time around law enforcement—especially on the range during qualifications—knows that just because someone is a cop, does not mean they can shoot well. In fact, it is well known that a great majority of officers only shoot when they are told that they *have* to, such as for qualifications, and that can be as little as 25 to 50 rounds a year. These two occupations, LE and military, do not guarantee skill with firearms.

Another key point about the military: when it comes to handguns a majority of military assignments do not offer the recruit much handgun training at all. Again, *the majority of military personnel do not receive any handgun training beyond very basic qualifications, if that*. Many people simply do not know this. Unless you are an MP, an officer or some type of specialist, you are a soldier and your weapon is a rifle.

There's also the fact that a very small percentage of military actually deploy into a war zone, and an even smaller percentage of them actually see fighting up close. Keep this in mind the next time someone mentions that their buddy who just got back from a combat zone could teach all of you how to shoot handguns for civilian self-defense purposes. I'm not saying that he can't. *What I am saying is that you do not know if he actually can*.

Another problem with blind respect that needs pointed out, and this will go a long way in helping your situational awareness and mindset as well: Rule #1 about people: People are people. Period. No matter where they are, or what they have done, they are still just people. What this means is that in any group of people from society as a whole, to occupations, and even to specialists, you have:

- people who are great at what they do
- people who are good enough to get by
- people who downright suck
- and literally everything in between

I don't care if we're talking about doctors, lawyers, soldiers, cops…it doesn't matter. People do not cease being fallible, quirky human beings just because they don a uniform, pass a test or follow orders. Some are nutty, some are calm, some are intense, and sadly some are plain stupid. They carry these characteristics into every occupation with them.

While the willingness to put on a uniform and go into harm's way itself is deserving of great respect, it does not automatically indicate that they have excelled in any particular skill levels with guns *or their ability to teach gun fighting and self-defense in a civilian or domestic law enforcement context*. This is especially true when it comes to firearms training because, as I have witnessed repeatedly, not every one of them can shoot very well. This does not change as you move higher up the rank, either. I have trained with some SWAT operators who were top-notch serious shooters who train with the most up-to-date backflow of special operations information and TTP's coming back from the field of war and who send thousands of rounds a year down range practicing them. Conversely, I've worked in law enforcement supply and encountered several guys who are legitimately on SWAT teams and literally couldn't tell you what generation the Glock on their hip is, or why their rifle-to-pistol transitions are terrible as they struggle with the toy sling that shipped with their $600 hobby-grade carbine. These are real conversations I have personally had with "SWAT" officers.

The same goes for military. I've trained many guys who have served in the military how to shoot handguns. Most of them freely admit that they have very little handgun experience. I know a Ranger, who since leaving the military, hasn't touched a gun in 20 years. Aside from losing the perishable skill and knowledge of shooting, think about how much the training, skills, tactics and methodologies have changed in 20 years. The point is, just because he has a Ranger tab and spent a few years carrying a gun in South America 20 years ago, doesn't mean that, today right here and right now, he is the most qualified to teach you handgun use for civilian self-defense. Especially when he hasn't even owned a gun in 20 years.

And remember, just because someone is SWAT, or ex-mil, doesn't mean they actually were ever in a fight, or have much experience with the solo, up close and personal type of fighting you need to prepare for. The world of civilian criminal violence is very different than military engagements in a foreign country, with the entire might of the U.S. government supplying you. And even though LE and SWAT deal with the same criminals, they are still entering the situation typically with a *disparity of force* greatly on their side. They rarely get into a gunfight that they didn't go into with an overwhelming amount of force and equipment advantage on their side. Nor do they go in as rookies without experienced guidance. Patrol rookies do ride along, and special operations teams always have experienced guys leading the way. None of that is not going to be the case when you face the criminal alone out there. So, keep that in perspective. Also, let's not forget about those considerations of rules, parameters and consequences of *civilian* violence and self-defense. neither military nor law enforcement are trained as civilians facing those consequences. It's not that they can't know or learn them, but they are definitely not inherently part of their job training.

Special forces and special operations guys can be a bit different and are often very highly skilled in small arms and close combat. However, I've met more than a few special operations guys who, at the end of the day, are knuckle-dragging war machines and the best of the best when it comes to going somewhere and professionally breaking shit. However, these same men would straight up suck at trying to teach a low-skilled civilian anything (and would probably freak out from the low-speed drag you'd put them through.)

The examples are endless, but you get the idea. It's not the profession or the credential, it's the person, and their own personal dedication to the skill set in question *coupled with their ability to teach it well.* Now, before you launch a hate attack on me for saying anything but absolute praise about military and police personnel, understand that none of the above is said with malice. In fact, a lot of the best training I have personally had has come from LE and ex-mil instructors who are phenomenal at fighting *and* teaching. But these guys are the *exception* by the sheer number of law enforcement and ex-mil people that are out there.

In their defense, you should also understand that there are reasons for the skills of military and police being lower than we would expect them to be. One huge problem is the lack of funding for training and ammunition in both fields. Police and military have both experienced and unending trend of reduced budgets. Those reductions in budgets unfortunately always cut training near the top of the list. Having worked in police supply and at an LEO owned firing range, I have heard countless stories of departments having zero training outside of their yearly qualifications. Sadly, I would say it is the norm. I've also heard veterans describe the lack of ammunition allocated to training time as well during their time in service (while others describe a surplus).

So, while it is true that some people are just half-asses no matter what their occupation is, the main problem with these government forces is the lack of funding and the lack of a philosophy that prioritizes quality, live-fire training. I have also heard quite a few stories of departments with huge ammo stocks and open range times that can't get their officers to even go and shoot for free. But, free or not, at the end of the day the guy who is serious about being damn good is going to train. He will do it because he loves it. He will do it because he wants to live, *even if it comes out of his own pocket.*

Police and Military: Disparity of Force

The greatest difference between the experience of veteran military and law enforcement personnel and civilian needs is known as *disparity of force.* This is the one area that absolutely sets even the most experienced cop or warfighter apart from the needs of a civilian for defense against criminal violence. Disparity of Force is the ultimate advantage that is nearly always leveraged against the enemy or suspect by organized units and personnel.

The components of advantage can be broken into two distinct groups: support, and experience. Support is a huge advantage that the cop and warfighter will have for most of their career above what a civilian will ever have to work with. The LEO and the soldier are funded by the taxpayer, equipped weapons, communications, vehicles, armor, artillery and air support, backup on call, and basically any gadget or implement that makes their fight capabilities well above the enemy they will face. When you have the entire weight of the government behind you, you can go into a gunfight with a pretty good amount of confidence in how well you are equipped and supported in every way. Understand, I am not saying that it is a perfect situation for all of them, and I am definitely aware that there are always areas for improvement wherever bureaucracy is involved. However, when compared to the lone civilian just going about daily life, the disparity in support is tremendous.

The second component, experience, is also very important. Not only do military and police typically receive training, equipment, backup and logistical support, they almost never go into hot situations as rookies without being accompanied by someone who is experienced to lead them. This is critical. As a civilian, when you have your first engagement in deadly force, how nice would it be to have someone there with you who has done it before to guide the operation? This is exactly how agencies and branches of military tend to operate in smaller unit special operations. There is always someone there who has done it before, who will lead by example.

Civilians (or the small town or rural cop) simply will never have that benefit in a criminal violence situation. What this means is that the military or police instructor you are learning from may have never been on his own, like you will have to be. I'm not saying at all that they can't understand this and adapt their experience and teaching to your needs. But, if someone has never been specifically trained to handle solo self-defense without support, experienced leaders or vast equipment advantage, then it must be acknowledged that their experience is, while still relevant, outside of the lane we are talking about. Lonely civilian defense against criminal violence is a unique experience.

The Credential Adopters

The last guy you ever want to train with is the notorious "credential by proxy" guy, who adopts the credential of someone he took classes off of. Just because you took some training off of a SEAL or Delta guy, does not mean you get to put that on your resume as "SEAL trained" or "Delta Force trained." Yes, I have seen this. I once saw a guy hang his shingle to do concealed carry certification courses (required by my State to get your license), and his main advertisement said, "Navy SEAL trained instructor". While he may have trained with some SEAL's in a number of open enrollment classes, is he lying? Well, not exactly. However, it's cheesy as hell to be so misleading and adopt someone else's credentials into your own. You might not be lying, but you are being misleading as fuck. In the end, you are not a SEAL, or whoever you are trying to attach yourself to. Beware of schools or instructors that advertise themselves this way.

Professional Student/Competition Shooter

This is the one who has great shooting and gun manipulation skills and lots of civilian training. They may have trained with most of the famous instructors around the nation. They've got the cool gear, picture perfect draw strokes and maybe some sweet you tube videos. They may have a phenomenal competition record and could even be world famous. What they probably don't have is any real experience with violence or violent people. Can you learn to shoot from them? Sure, you can, and probably better than from anyone else. But that does not mean they will give you your money's worth in *self-defense training*. The lack of any experiential understanding of violence and its consequences is a serious gap in their knowledge.

These instructors are great for shooting technique, not so great for actual violence considerations or mindset. As a result, much of what they teach about "fighting" is often pure choreography and ritual, neither of which will help you in an unpredictable and fluid fight. Be cautious here if they package themselves as the *complete package* of comprehensive self-defense instruction when in reality they are only offering the shooting components. While they are extremely fortunate to have not led a life tainted by the pain and misery of violence, they are consequently not equipped to offer a complete package for self-defense training

I'd like to touch on the combatives side of training here as well. Since the domination of Brazilian Jiu Jitsu in the world of martial arts, the argument of "street ready" martial arts have taken a much more complex form. While the competition shooter may be clearly seen as not having been a real gunfighter, it is much harder to differentiate between a martial artist who has done real fighting and one who hasn't. In that world, claims about "street ready" technique abound. While this could be a book in itself, I'd like to address one main claim here: *"if it was on the streets it would have ended differently."* That statement is both true and false; it totally depends on who is saying it. There are different types of violence. Fighting that is not driven by the desire to murder and maim is more of a challenge of skill and technique. So, when "that would have ended differently on the streets" is touted by someone who is not a killer, it is false. They wouldn't fight any fucking differently on the street than they would in the gym, and if they lost in the gym, they're simply making excuses.

However, there are some people who would be telling the truth if they said, "it would have ended differently out there." Real killers. The truly violent obviously cannot use what they really know in a "friendly" match on the mat. But, if they tell you that it would be different on the streets, you can bet your ass it would be very different. There are some people out there who have a very low degree of skill in competition or "friendly" fighting, but are extremely effective in murderous level violence and ambush. This is such a hard concept to get across to people who have not experienced it. It's just hard to understand if you believe you possess the highest level of violence, yet you are not a steely-eyed killer (or at least have fought one or two along the way).

My point here is to keep in mind that competition and real violence are two very different things. The mindset of the extremely violent criminal is what you should get to know. If you begin to learn what that is like, the difference between the "friendly" competition and murder become very apparent. I have no desire to engage in debates about this. I have done both. I just want you, the student, to think about it deeply when considering information gained from others. In the end, when it comes to *isolated skills and techniques*, the competition guys are the most highly developed.

Just keep an eye out for the loud guy who has no real-world experience and talks incessantly about how many hours of training he has had as an instructor and student of *the way*.

The Fudd

The Fudd, on the other hand, is a particular pet peeve of mine in the concealed carry world. Aptly named after Elmer Fudd, they are the typical, older "gun guy" who has hunted most if not all of his life, thinks the world revolves around the NRA's training modules, and has absolutely zero background in any type of combat shooting (outside of maybe some IDPA matches or the bad police training of the 70's and 80's). You can't tell them a *damn thing* about guns and shooting. They love snub nose revolvers, and they love to push brand-new shooters, and everyone else, into snubbie revolvers. A Fudd can be a retired cop, the guy at the gun and hunting club, and shockingly they can be a younger version emulating the original Fudds. They will almost universally teach pure NRA Basic Pistol courses as concealed carry, which I find absolutely maddening because a recreation shooting course should not be used as a self-defense course. Back when I used to teach it, I can't count how many of my own Alumni started their training with me by taking my concealed carry course despite having taken a Fudd's course prior to mine. Unanimously they all state the same thing, "This is completely different than anything I learned in the first class!" Of course, it is. If you are serious about combat/self-defense shooting, don't waste your money with a Fudd. If you want to learn trapshooting, or maybe bullseye, then the Fudd is your man.

The Character of an Instructor

Let me be clear about something: I do not have an adversarial attitude toward other quality instructors. In fact, I have found that most *quality* instructors feel the same way. My experience with them has been very positive and even when I was just considering getting into the business many were helpful and supportive. And when my popularity rose, they didn't turn on me. This stands out to me because it is not always the case with the instructor-to-instructor relationship; I have had some bad experiences. I would say that in 99.9% of those negative interactions, the instructors were local, mainly taught the state mandated course, and were clearly subpar. I believe wholeheartedly that how an instructor views, relates to, or talks about other reputable instructors is a telling clue about their worth as a teacher. I also view the job we do as firearms instructors as being one of the strongest points of activism for the Second Amendment and the right to self-defense.

The lobbying organizations and civil rights groups would not exist without a grassroots base. When you properly instruct someone, they don't just go home with a CCW certificate or a general knowledge of gun safety; they become a shooter. They support the industry, buy guns and ammo, practice, and expose others to the shooting world from a more positive angle. The increased knowledge and experience out there puts more pressure on manufacturers to stop pushing so much junk. You are adding to the grassroots base and strengthening the fabric of social order by contributing to the amount of well-armed, well-trained advocates of self-defense out there. This goes for LE instructors as well. The difference between a well-trained officer and a poorly trained officer will eventually be the difference between a good day and horrible catastrophe. We all make a difference.

The more closed-minded someone is, the less they will learn and the less they can pass on. Having an adversarial attitude toward other instructors is not an admirable quality and prohibits you from learning anything. Trust me, you don't know *everything*. If you are afraid of being "bested" or one-upped on the range...that's precisely the reason to get more training, not avoid it. If you can be easily one-upped on the range, then you can also be easily one-upped on the street where there are no second-place trophies. It's only an "instructor competition" if you make it one, and the ones who do make it a competition tend to avoid giving someone the opportunity to beat them at it. That speaks volumes. Think back to the standards section, and realize that you are a product of your own standards.

An instructor should be a student. I consider it an OBLIGATION to constantly pursue the highest levels of training for myself and my instructors for my company. But even if the instruction doesn't introduce many new things to us, it's a chance to get out and shoot in the style that we train in and assess our own skills in comparison to other serious shooters. It's a chance to take style notes from someone who was at least good enough to entice *you* away from your time and money. Why pass that up? I, for one, certainly will not let an ego problem get between me and a day on the range with shooters as good as (and hopefully better than) I am. And if you only spend time around people who are not as good as you, you'll never know how good you can really be.

So how do you begin to pick a good instructor? A quick scrutiny of a few readily available things like: reputation, content/presence on the internet, and a conversation (if you know what to ask); if they pass these tests, then you give them the final exam: take a class with them. You'll see right away what they're about. But if you choose them solely based on things like flashy moves, clinical vocabularies, or what uniform they wear/wore, you're probably doing it wrong. You might get lucky, or you might just get bad information. The instructor MUST be able to explain WHY a skill or technique is used, and should offer that information without prompting. The teaching should be based upon *principles*, and those principles should serve the *specific* purpose of winning a civilian-level violent criminal confrontation including all of the subsequent consequences. Most importantly, you need to understand that instructors who have the entire package are extremely rare.

Finding someone like this means they will have *all* of the following: great fighting *and* shooting skills, valuable real-world experience in *civilian violence* and everything that goes with it (physical, legal, psychological and social), a great understanding of an all-encompassing self-defense mindset and, on top of all of that, great abilities to teach these rare things to beginners. That is a lot to ask for in one person. The men or women who possess all of these at once are out there, but are *very* rare. In your search for training in these matters, you will most likely have to sit at the feet of several teachers and there is nothing wrong with that. Just remember this when you run across the guy selling you "everything you ever need to know to win a gunfight" training. I honestly have to say that I do not think anyone has ALL of the answers. No one person has encountered or even thought of ALL of the problems that can arise. Therefore, it's impossible to possess "the magic cube" of answers. None of us know "the one true way" to do anything technically or tactically. There is no such thing as *the one true way* in violence. Yes, there are some definite wrong ways to do things, no argument there. But all *quality* instruction will have something good; tools to put in your defensive toolbox.

The more you have in that toolbox, the more prepared you are for unpredictable and diverse situations. The techniques or tactics you learn from the Delta Force guy will be different than what the State SWAT instructor shows you; the Force Recon vet will introduce different perspectives than the federal weapons instructor. And you can bet that the guy who has never deployed in military or law enforcement but has taught hundreds or thousands of competition/combat shooting students has a few things to show you as well (Jerry Miculek). And don't forget the rare crossovers like myself who can give you direct insight into criminal violence, which IS what you are preparing for. Quality instructors are not a dime a dozen, but they do come in many flavors and from diverse backgrounds. If you have chosen to pursue firearms and combatives training for civilian defensive purposes, take your time and seek the best information out across a variety of perspectives. Don't look at a competition record, belt, job or uniform as a standard for quality.

One very important thing to remember is this: square range training is not fight training. Too many confuse this. Decision making and solving fast moving problems *is* fighting. Therefore, training for that requires an immense of amount of experience to design and guide the student into that clear decision-making process. It's learning to operate intuitively at the procedural level. Decision making, procedures, intuitive recognition of problems and the governing principles outside of specific circumstances, footwork, momentum, rules of engagement, priority of life, advanced safety and the conditioning to be able to perform within all of it...this is just a scratch on the surface of conscious and unconscious fight capabilities.

Big words, "scientific" explanations, big marketing budgets, flashy productions, popularity, years in the selling business and impressive shooting skills...these are not what are most important IF your goal is to learn how to fight. Validation does exist. My only caution to you is to not think you've got the world by the ass when it comes to understanding what fighting is and how to train for it. The tool doesn't matter. It's 10% of a fight. The rest is problem solving with clear decision making and executing on those decisions decisively and correctly.

SECTION THREE: CONDITIONING AND ORIENTATION

CHAPTER NINE: CONDITIONING

The journey from learning skills to becoming a fighter

The two major components of the framework of training, as I see it, are conditioning and orientation. Training should have the primary goal of developing these two components in the fighter. Conditioning includes both the physical conditioning to perform skills on demand and with endurance, and developing the mental ability to both assess problems and persevere in the face of extreme adversity.

Conditioning comes through dedicated training, repeated exposure, and study. Orientation is the basis for mindset. Your response to violence will be based upon your orientation to the violent situation. Your conditioning and confidence level, your attachments in life, your cultural beliefs (particularly about violence), and ultimately your real experience level, all make up your orientation. Through these experiences and beliefs, you will make a series of decisions which will determine how you will assess and respond to a violent encounter.

In one of my worst engagements, the stabbing I was convicted for, I experienced auditory and visual exclusion to a very high degree. I stabbed my opponent in the presence of 2 of his accomplices, and about 8 witnesses. There were screams, yelling, threats, etc. and I heard none of it all the way through stabbing him over 20 times. When I ended up in prison as a result, the atmosphere was much more volatile, and onlookers became much more dangerous. Therefore, out of necessity I had to develop the ability to remain aware of my surroundings regardless of how terrible the fight that I was in became.

This ability develops in those who are capable of developing this. Those who couldn't, suffered. Some paid the ultimate price. This is orientation at work, and you cannot mimic that in the gym or on the range. Not fully. But, you can work in the right direction, through properly designed conditioning and study. One of the most frustrating things as an instructor has been to get people to stop seeing everything as a "training" problem and to start seeing it as an orientation problem. The physical stuff is the fun stuff. It's tangible. It makes great Instagram accounts. But the understanding and discipline for actual conditioning work is rarely there.

There are two types of conditioning: physical (as in fitness or athletic conditioning) and psychological (as in classical or operant stimulus response conditioning). Both apply to our subject matter, but I will deal with the psychological aspect of conditioning primarily in the "Orientation" chapter of the book. For now, let's look at the subject of physical conditioning.

PHYSICAL CONDITIONING

Developing the delivery system of skills and decisions

Physical conditioning, in my experience, accomplishes two main goals: First, it develops the skills, techniques and principles of the fundamental capabilities needed to fight. Simultaneously, it builds the strength, speed and endurance of the physical carriage to deliver those skills learned in training or from primal instinct. Another very important result of proper conditioning is that it also improves the ability to process information and make decisions in the face of changing variables and circumstances. That is the essential part of fighting capabilities that so many miss out on if their training does not include a serious conditioning program, both for the skills and for fitness. That part can begin to happen through simply training the fundamentals until they are intuitive and applicable with either creativity or specificity.

By knowing the skill so well that you can both decide to use it *and* use it without conscious thought, you free up your conscious thought process allowing you to better analyze real-time information and make better decisions based on that information. But the physical capabilities part only comes through repetitive, challenging work and confidence testing (validation).

Improving your strength, mobility and stability for fighting in ambush/counter-ambush situations is not widely understood, nor is it promoted in the training world enough. In classes, I see more people that have zero idea of how to actually move their bodies into and out of positions for fighting, than people that do. I know that sounds like such a simple statement, but it never fails to give people a reality check when they attend their first firearms class that includes basic level hands-on fighting concepts, as some of mine do, and they quickly realize that they never had a clue as to how to actually engage in a physical fight with someone. Or, and often simultaneously, they realize that their physical condition is nowhere near what is needed to perform the tasks they have as their current plan. They *adopted a plan of action and never tested it*. In other words, many people just believe they will grapple and/or shoot and win. Then when put up against pressure testing, they learn that not one part of that plan was properly prepared for. They are walking around with an untested hypothesis for a plan to save their life.

SKILLS TRAINING

Firearms and Combatives

Firearms skills cannot be learned from a book completely, or very well. Nor would I want to create a text that can travel the world and teach how to do it, regardless of who they are, good or bad. I just want to talk about the approach to weapons training that I use and how to apply it in the context of your mission. To learn specific skills and drills, get to a class.

Skills practice can be wasted if not done for the express purpose of conditioning. When a musician puts in time on their instrument, they are not only practicing the notes and patterns, they are conditioning the muscles involved in playing the instrument. The continuous practice is also creating the myelination of the nerve pathways involved in sending the signals to the muscles for the precise movements. After some serious time in practice and immersion, the musician can perform the precise moves without conscious thought.

At an even later point, improvisation becomes possible as the musician can begin to randomly perform the precise moves to create patterns that are unrehearsed and unplanned, or that are in response to other musicians leading the improv. This is the result of proper conditioning. That point where fundamental skills cross over and become a personalized technique that naturally occurs. This is how Eric Clapton and Stevie Ray Vaughan could have picked up the exact same Stratocaster, but perform incredibly different tones and phrases from it. That is the result of conditioning. The fundamental skills of pressing a note, bending a string to pitch, playing a scale, all come together to be blended into unique, personalized music. Yes, creativity is the higher level of performance.

The fighter is no different here. The practice of skills cannot simply conclude with the performance of those isolated skills. The fighter must reach a point where the skills are completely owned and wired into the brain as selectable messages that can be combined or modified to fit the current circumstance. And this is the precise point where fighting styles fail. Traditional styles of fighting created "canned and planned" responses, and push the perfection of those responses as a way of marking achievement.

While this is fine for the art or rule-driven sport, it is not sufficient for the demands of uncontrolled circumstances. For environments where things change rapidly, and one cannot possibly prepare for every unpredictable variable, adaptability must be in the fighter's abilities. The goal: Conditioning the fundamental skills into a repertoire of tasks that can be creatively and intuitively combined, on demand and without prior planning, for responding to an unpredictable circumstance. This is the goal of skills practice.

Let's take the handgun draw for example. We can debate about whether we should draw up to eye level and press out, or whether we should flip muzzle to target as soon as we clear the holster and drive it up at an angle to eye level, but the underlying purpose of the move is to get the damn gun out and place accurate shots on the target. So, however you choose to practice it, you need to keep in mind that variables will change. You may not have time to get the gun up to eye level, grasp with two hands, and press it out to a clean sight picture. Hell, you may have to go one-handed. So, the difference is between learning the draw stroke as a regimented form that *must be* performed this particular way *because someone said so*, versus getting the gun out and efficiently and safely getting hits on the preferred area regardless of circumstances or form.

How is this achieved? For me, it is by first learning a form, and then conditioning that form to the point that you actually understand the underlying principles of time, efficiency and safety, and that they are *for all intents and purposes independent of that strict form*. In other words, *proper* conditioning is a type of training that uses forms to learn the basics, and then deconstructs the fighter's reliance on those forms in favor of understanding the objectives of the movements and achieving those objectives through the creative application of capabilities regardless of environmental circumstances.

This is *next level* knowledge. This is what lies beyond kata and choreography and exists in the realm of accomplishment and adaptability. And guess what? This is the type of thing that your enemy understands intuitively and has trained at on the streets and in prison. Watch interviews with defected gang members and known killers with high body counts. They will explain this process to you with such simplicity that most people won't even catch it; it slides right by the average person. I know because, in many ways, I am one of them. When the necessity of being good at something is driven by life or death outcomes, human beings are incredibly adaptable and will excel at performing through exposure, mental rehearsal and practice. The ones who can't, die.

The successful will always, in those high stakes environments, eliminate all fluff and unnecessary decisions and movements and just get the job done as simply as possible.

To understand this further, one of the things that I teach on the range is that your ultimate physical goal as a gunfighter is to be able to run your gun in any position you find yourself in, and within any circumstances affecting you. This of course takes into account the immense amount of emphasis I put into making good decisions and performing within the principles of time, efficiency, strength, mobility, stability and advanced safety. It is complex. Too complex to rely on rehearsal or memory to perform pre-planned "moves" or forms. You must achieve an intuitive understanding of the capabilities and how they can be applied to achieve underlying objectives. This is where the rubber meets the road.

Training the physical skills in fighting, be it weapons based or empty handed, should be approached through conditioning rather than rehearsal. This is a difficult concept to grasp at first, until one begins to develop that naturally occurring technique. It is at that point adaptability begins to shine through and the reliance on strict forms and specific circumstances falls away. The fighter emerges, ready to adapt with the creative application of skills, techniques and procedures based on an intuitive understanding of the objectives and principles of the task.

How do we condition skills?

Your training should consist of so much practice of isolated skills that they become nearly automatic and require little to no conscious thought to perform. At this point, you must begin to move away from the strict form and challenge yourself to come up with unorthodox ways to achieve the objective. For example, take away the picture perfect, sunny day, square range draw stroke and add another person whom you must protect and evacuate. Now, one hand may be involved in pushing or driving the innocent out of harm's way while the other is clearing garments and retrieving the weapon. Throughout all of this, you must be able to

155

move yourself, the innocent, and deploy the weapon while achieving accurate hits in the preferred area while not causing any other unintended harm.

This is just one example of innumerable variables that can be used to challenge your adherence to strict forms. Altering clothing, creating obstacles, limiting yourself to one hand, initiating the draw from a vehicle seat, or from laying on the ground...these are other ways to make it happen. This should be practiced first with inert training guns, airsoft, or laser, because at this point it becomes much more dangerous as mistakes and stress go in hand-in-hand here. Once you begin to find ways to achieve the objective while adhering to the principles, you can begin to seek validation through pressure testing and force-on-force. It really is not as beneficial to go to a validation course, and wrestle with opponents, if you have no idea of how to achieve objectives through less than ideal circumstances. Sure, you can learn on the fly, but you will get so much more out of it if you are introduced to the basic underlying principles and how to use them to achieve objectives regardless of circumstances.

There are two very common mistakes in training:
- Focusing on learning skills and techniques without putting in the work of conditioning
- Seeking validation without putting in the prior work of conditioning

Everyone wants to do the minimum, yet reap the maximum reward. One of the more popular "fighting movies" of today is the John Wick series. Guys secretly want to be Mr. Wick. But, you can't fight like John Wick, unless you train like John Wick. Specifically, Keanu Reeves spent a few months training on the range 4 times a week firing 1000 to 1500 rounds a day working under a competition champion for his shooting skill. He spent countless hours with a counter-terrorist concealment specialist and consultant working on concealment and concealed weapon technique. He trained 5 to 6 days a week in Japanese jiu jitsu,

Brazilian jiu jitsu, judo, tactical shooting, 3-gun competition shooting, concealment technique. He did this under the guidance of some of the best in those respective disciplines, day in and day out, for more than a few months. High frequency training is a most sure path of conditioning. That was his job, just so he could *act* like he knew it.

I am sure that you cannot quit your job today and go hire all of these top-level trainers and consultants to begin a boot camp style of full time training for months on end. And even if you could, it still would not make you an actual fighter in a few months. Even at this extreme rate of full immersion training, Reeves is not an *experienced* fighter, and you would not be either. Yet, many think they can take a weekend class every few months and spend a few hours in the gym a week and they're going to be able to walk into a full-blown validation and perform like a boss.

The problem is exacerbated when nearly everyone else at that validation is like you, so you actually perform pretty good against them. This is false confidence. Just because you can successfully win a mock gunfight in a class, or wrestle a gun away from another average joe student, does not make you an accomplished fighter prepared for whatever the criminal world has to throw at you. It's a good little test to give you a taste of the demands of fighting, but without actual conditioning work, you don't improve or own any of that required skill. (I want to remind you here that I am not saying that every American needs to train to the level of a pro athlete in order to defend themselves. I am talking here specifically about those who want to take it seriously enough to pursue high performance and professionalism.)

Specifically working to improve your strength, speed and endurance while also pursuing the repetitive practice of skills and techniques is the driving force of conditioning. The higher the frequency of practice the better you will become at it, and the better your body will be prepared to deliver it. Something magical happens when you put in the work and own the skills. You become intuitive about problem solving and how to use your body to accomplish solutions. For example, watch people on the range who have some fighting or martial arts background. They will move and change positions much quicker and smoother than the others. They have learned at least a little bit how to get their bodies from one position to another and specifically doing it to solve problems. This is just a small piece of that big puzzle.

CHAPTER TEN: ORIENTATION

ORIENTATION IS THE FOUNDATION OF MINDSET

Mindset is ultimately the reason I got into the business of teaching self-defense and violence education. When I participated in self-defense training, whether in combatives or gun fighting, I learned that there was not any real mindset content being taught that I found to be realistic or experience based, at least in the civilian and law enforcement communities I trained in. Everybody and their third cousin was teaching skills-based classes, with not much of the important stuff to go along with it. Since I had obviously survived a whole bunch of really violent shit without this formal training, I came to the conclusion that your mindset at any given moment is more important than what skills you do or do not have. If you cannot correctly process information and make good decisions, nothing else will help you.

Your orientation is the collection of building blocks that construct your mindset. It is made up of all of the values and perceptions that you will process your decisions through. How you feel about violence culturally, what your personal values are, the attachments that drive your mission, the parameters of your mission, your experience level and your confidence are all what make up your orientation. It is vitally important to understand how these values, beliefs and perceptions shape your decision making, because *decision making is the product of mindset*.

It is also critical that you apply the two-way principle here: what governs you is what also governs the enemy. They have an orientation as well, that is built by the same components. In this book, we are dealing specifically with the criminal element, so their orientation filters will be quite different than yours. It has been taught in warrior culture for thousands of years, "to know yourself, is to know your enemy." Only through conquering yourself can you achieve victory in conquering a dedicated opponent. Here, we are going to take a deep introductory look at how to build a strong orientation that can be relied upon to construct the mindset needed when facing severe adversity.

The values, attachments and parameters that we use to make every decision act like filters that ultimately influence our thoughts about an event. We can begin to break down those decision filters as follows:

- Culture
- Values
- Attachments
- Parameters
- Experience
- Confidence

Culture

Culture plays a huge role in your orientation. In the simplest example, if you culturally are against violence, you will have a hard time performing violence. Many of you may have been raised to strongly believe that violence is wrong. It is just simply not socially acceptable to be violent according to most cultural influences in the United States. However, your enemy does not feel that way. They are most often raised where violence is not only acceptable, it is the primary way to power and prestige. It is also a primary tool in gaining what is desired, hence the armed robbery, armed carjacking, muggings and violent home invasions.

If you were raised, or somehow believe that violence is not acceptable, it will take a lot of work for you to overcome that. The danger here is that you can lull yourself into believing that you are "OK" with it; that you could perform it without hesitation *if needed*. The problem comes when you actually have to a) accept that another human being is trying to mortally wound you, and b) mortally wound another human being. You may find that it is more

160

difficult to be dedicated to lethal force against a human than you thought it was. You can fear the legal or social consequences. You can fear judgement of a higher power, God, or family members you love. You can fear the *finality* of putting holes in another living being. Think about some decisions you've made in life that you knew would be irreversibly life-changing, and how you stressed over the finality of them. Imagine having to do that in a split-second decision knowing that you may end someone's life in front of your own eyes, and that it will then change you and your life forever. This requires very deep thought long before that moment comes.

There are many things that can attack your confidence through your cultural influences that will place negative mental images in your mind at the precise moment you really need to have confidence and certainty in your success. Your enemy, conversely, will not only not have those same cultural limitations, he will have cultural beliefs and experience that will reinforce his confidence and certainty. He has (in many cases) experienced extreme violence his whole life. He is very likely to have vastly more experience committing violence against other human beings than you ever will. This means he will be much quicker and much more confident in decision making. He is a predator in touch with his predator instincts through environmental and cultural conditioning. You, on the other hand, are the result of hundreds of years of modern civilization breeding the predator instinct out of you with the trappings of comfort, agriculture and grocery, technology and civility; the illusions of safety and security.

Your inner predator needs reawakened. The most effective way to alter a cultural belief or set of principles is through necessity. If you do not first realize that it is sometimes necessary to meet force with force, aggression with greater aggression, you cannot be properly motivated to change deep seated beliefs or values. Only through necessity will we, as creatures of habit, begin to change. Necessity increases the importance of any information that is involved in the solution of a new problem or realization that is causing the necessity. As the information becomes more important to you, your ability to retain and synthesize that new information increases greatly.

When we realize how necessary our use of force can be, and how important it is that we be both prepared and willing to use that force, we will learn, and we will change. This is why, sadly, too many people only come for serious training and help after something bad has already happened to them or someone they love.

Begin by studying two main sources: people who have done violence in defense or as a job and are willing to share and articulate their experiences, and criminals who have done violence and are saying how they felt about doing it (such as the shows and interviews where they talk to violent inmates and death row convicts). Knowing your enemy thoroughly will create a sense of necessity in you. Listening to the stories of other "good guys" who have taken life or have been involved in extreme violence will begin to help you prioritize what is important in your belief system.

Values

Your values are the standards and personal principles that govern your behavior. How you see the world and treat others is based on your values and what you deem to be important in life. Do you always try to see the good in others? Do you try to be fair and honest, regardless of the other person's behavior? These values must be identified and, in some cases, separated from the decisions you use in violence. I know it sounds senseless, but it is possible during a fight to have compassion on an attacker, especially at the precise moment you have a chance to mortally wound them. You may, at that moment, think about giving them a chance and may even fool yourself into believing it would end well for you.

But make no mistake about it, if you did not initiate or escalate the conflict, and were senselessly attacked in a violent way to the point that you or someone you care about is in mortal danger, then that attacker deserves no further consideration. This will be in stark contrast to the value system you have lived with all of your life. If you do not directly recognize and address this, you will be in serious trouble during or after a conflict. There are countless stories of police officers experiencing similar feelings as well, if they weren't particularly oriented towards violence, so it applies to working professionals as much as civilians. Remember, one of our main goals is to be a professional, whether you are a civilian or you get paid to do it doesn't matter.

Conversely, if you typically dislike people and distrust them, your decision making during violence will also be affected negatively and you can easily go overboard in your response. I have observed throughout my years in hostile places around hostile people, that people typically fight the way that they communicate. Because both are filtered through the same decision-making processes and value systems in dealing with people.

If you have someone who is quick to anger during verbal exchanges, typically they will be an angry fighter, and so on. The strategic will fight strategically. The thoughtful will outsmart if they can. It has just held true whenever I have been able to witness both. This is also something very well known to a predator, instinctually. It is very easy and reliable to predict an average person's violence response based on how they are communicating. Most people do not ever have the opportunities I had to observe those who I would have to fight someday over long periods of time in close proximity to each other. This experience should not be overlooked in its importance to you as I am sharing it with you. I have both observed predators in their daily life, and fought them.

The role that values play in mindset and overall orientation is huge. It is critical to recognize the extent to which your value system will affect your decision-making processes during violence. The product of mindset is decision making. The product of a strong mindset is good decision making under all conditions. Your ability to maintain self-control and make good decisions starts with applying the proper values to the questions developing in your mind. Trying to suddenly apply a value system that comes from a

163

"peaceful" paradigm during a violent encounter will create confusion for you. Confusion leads to uncertainty, the enemy of confidence.

Attachments

Plainly stated, your "attachments" are what motivate you most in decision making, especially during violent confrontations. Attachments are your greatest motivators and also your greatest source of fear. In many cases, you will only experience stark fear when something you are deeply attached to is threatened. For example, you are attached to your own life and well-being; you do not want to die or be maimed. You may also be deeply attached to your loved ones and your comfortable life. This can be both a source of fear and a motivator. Without taking a close look at our attachments, we are unable to truly begin to discipline our minds for self-control when those attachments become threatened.

When we understand that it is our own attachments that both motivate and hinder us, we can begin to cultivate a mindset around those attachments that will put them in their proper place and allow us *to function independent of them* precisely when we need to execute on a decision.

What I mean by this is we can understand what it is that we are fighting for, giving it the proper priority of importance, and then set it aside so we can do our job to protect it. It is when we become focused on our attachments, or the thought of losing them, that anger, fear and uncertainty begin to take control. We cannot be effective fighters if we are busy allowing negative mental images about the loss of our attachments to attack our mind when we should be busy and focused on fighting.

As a kid in a violent home and upbringing, and as a young man in prison, I had very few attachments. I did not feel that same sense of clinging to family that average people fear. I actually hated my life as a kid, and had the attitude that "I didn't ask to be born into this fucking world, so why should I give a fuck?" This made me extremely dangerous. It lowered my fear greatly to sometimes imperceptible levels. It is how I came out on top in some of the deadly and dangerous situations I was involved in. Retrospectively, however, the greatest effect it had was that *it took the focus off of me and my inner world and put it directly on my opponent.*

Do you understand this? You NEED to know this about your enemy. When you are toiling away in your own mind worried about things that pertain to *you*, you are taking energy and focus away from your *enemy*. When you fought me as a kid or young man, you were fighting someone who absolutely didn't give a fuck about anything except hurting you, even if I died trying.

The most powerful example of understanding and controlling attachments can be learned from Gautama Buddha, the founder of Buddhism. Gautama learned of the limitations and disappointments of the world despite his father's great attempts to prevent that from happening. What Gautama deduced was, summarily, that all suffering stemmed from our attachments to things and ideas in this life. While I do not personally subscribe to the primary belief of relinquishing all attachments to end suffering, (I conversely believe that suffering brings growth and progress) I do believe there is a lot to be learned from a system dedicated to this one aspect of mindset and extreme self-control. Applying it to fighting, I transpose that concept to state that many of the pitfalls of a fighter--fear, anger, loss of control--are attributed to being fixated on our attachments *during the heat of the moment.*

Understanding that *extreme self-control under all conditions* is the goal, we can easily see how we must first clearly identify our attachments, what we are willing to do to protect them, and then put them in their proper place conclusively in our minds so that we can move on to completely focus on the tasks at hand. *We cannot protect something effectively by simply staring inward at it. We must look outward with our focus to be victorious as defenders.*

Parameters

The parameters of your mission are, to simplify it, what you are willing to do, what you are allowed to do, and what you are capable of doing. These are defined within your mission. I know this sounds like common sense, but not only do most people not have clearly identified parameters, they actually erroneously believe that they do.

For example, "that guy" on the internet or in a gun class that talks about shooting on sight anyone that comes uninvited into his home. This is a clear case of someone who has not identified boundaries and limitations, as is evidenced just by their making their sentiments of willfully killing people public. Not to mention the fact that what they are saying can be extremely incorrect depending on many circumstances.

When we step outside of the parameters of our mission, we make costly and even deadly mistakes. This is how fathers shoot their children dead in the middle of the night. This is how wives kill their husbands when they surprise them coming home early from a night shift. It happens all of the time, because someone did not understand that there are limitations to what is reasonable, legal and to what you are capable of doing.

Going flying into a deadly situation at full speed with a limited understanding of boundaries because you have not devoted critical thinking to them, will often end in tragedy. As an example, positive target identification is a boundary; a legal and moral boundary. In other words, you are running the greatest risk of all when you shoot at a figure and you do not clearly know who it is. Of course, this shooting in the home thing is just one example of countless scenarios where understanding boundaries will keep you out of trouble with lethal force.

How does this pertain to orientation and mindset? Because the parameters are more filters which you must process your decisions through in order to make good decisions in that moment. What can this cause? It can cause uncertainty. Uncertainty is the enemy of all fighters.

Think about it: being very certain and clear on what you are capable of doing, willing to do, and are allowed to do will boost your confidence in any situation. Lacking that information will produce the opposite effect. It will reduce your time out of the fight because there will be a whole set of questions that you will not be searching for an answer to. You will KNOW what you can and should do, so you can get busy doing it.

Experience

Nothing drives confidence like successful experience. Nothing. When we face a situation that we have faced before, or a situation even similar to something we have faced before, we have a much better idea about what to expect. This combats uncertainty. Previous experience will be one of the largest deciding filters we run our decisions through when we are faced with the fight. Experience can come in different forms:

- Real experience doing the exact thing, having been in deadly force situations
- Exposure: only having witnessed it happen to someone else
- Experience-by-proxy: learning directly from those who have experienced it
- Simulated experience: high-quality force-on-force training

Real experience obviously will have the most profound effect on you. However, it's important to note that it isn't always going to be a good effect. If you got hurt badly or otherwise were not successful, your uncertainty going into the next situation can be a deafening roar against your attempts to be calm and calculated. If you have been successful, it is much easier to pull on that experience to enter a situation with confidence. But if you were not successful, the only way you can muster confidence from it is to seek out the understanding of the reasons why you were not successful and to gain the training and capabilities to correct those problems.

I am a great case in point. I seek out training constantly, every year. Why do I do this, if I have won so many fights and survived so many deadly situations? Because, while I may have won the fights, I didn't always "win" the conflict. I paid dearly with nearly life-ruining consequences as a result of mistakes I made. This is why I teach this aspect so heavily in my coursework (*and how you learn through experience-by-proxy*). I needed to understand what I did wrong and find every possible way to avoid making those mistakes again.

What I found was that being the most violent guy in the fight is not how you "win". It can be precisely how you lose everything in the aftermath of violence. So, where I lacked good decision-making and strong fighting capabilities, I made up for it with sheer violence and brutality. Sheer violence and brutality send you to prison, no matter how "right" you are in defending yourself against an attack. Judging by the phrases that have become so cliché in this industry, too many people just do not understand the importance of this.

Exposure to violence can be very beneficial. It is what initiates the violence experience in most violent criminals. They are often raised in violent environments, like myself. The stress inoculation is unmatched, often times being desensitized to extreme violence by early adolescence. The orientation and value system is created around violence being an acceptable way to achieve ends, sometimes even glorified. It can also have a very negative effect on your confidence to deal with it. You can have a fear condition that is deeply ingrained from violent abuse, or from seeing someone you love fall victim to violence when you were incapable of helping. This is often seen in women who come from abusive environments or relationships. This must be overcome with understanding and conditioning through education and training.

Another unfortunate aspect of "exposure" is television violence. It is true that most Americans' exposure to violence comes from the news and movies, and the presentation is nowhere near factual or realistic in either case. As a matter of fact, this is the worst obstacle you will face in court, because you will sit being judged by people who have no real understanding of violence or what it really takes to stop a determined bad guy. If your only exposure to violence is from TV and movies, wipe your mind clean and start your education fresh. Get some quality training from nationally known and reputable instructors, and study real violent encounters on YouTube and other sources of surveillance footage from real scenes. This is how you can overcome the misconceptions of how it all works.

For most people, however, the only real experience you can achieve is simulated experience. This comes in the form of sparring and simulated firearms munitions training, known as force-on-force training. This is the absolute best way to find out what you can really do, to learn new capabilities, and to test what you learn against other real human attackers. This can't be a trip to a Mcdojo, or a weekend day at your local paintball range. I am talking about training and testing led by experienced and reputable professionals that follows a learning-based process with clear objectives.

I can't stress enough the importance of force-on-force training. If you are walking around carrying a gun for self-defense purposes, then you undoubtedly have some vision in your mind of how you will use that gun to respond to an attack. I can guarantee that if you have not had that "vision" tested, you are in for a great shock if you ever do. I have seen it over and over in force-on-force classes. People get their dreams and expectations crushed. It's a brutal wake-up call for most. When you know that the simulated ammunition in your opponent's gun can sting like a motherfucker, and may hurt you for a while (like getting hit in the hand ouch!), you get a realistic sense of what it's like to respond to an attacker that already has his gun out. You become aware of how quickly your gun and your quick draw skills will take a far back seat to your decision-making and mindset. It is better to find out in a class, than on the streets, where I have also seen many falls to that great shock of realizing how ineffective their untested plan was.

Confidence

Confidence is the culmination of all of the other components of orientation. How "self-aware" you are--how well you understand your cultural limitations, physical, moral and legal boundaries, your values and attachments, your experience and tested skills--will determine how confident you can be. It needs to be a true confidence; a confidence gained through training, study and conditioning, *and then tested*, is a confidence that is owned. Confidence is the product of proper orientation, and it is necessary in order to maintain extreme self-control under all conditions.

MENTAL CONDITIONING

For the orientation component, we need to understand how orientations are formed. We have two results from conditioning the orientation: adaptability, and mindset. When we grew up in violent atmospheres, suffering beatings, watching violence happen among loved ones, seeing them die, etc., we were *conditioned* to violence. In some ways we became desensitized, in others hardened and more focused. In that sense, the repeated exposure conditioned our paradigm, decision filters, and responses to such stimuli. We were taught that violence indisputably solves problems. We also received the reward of glory for violence abilities and achievements. This cannot be simply trained in a gym or on a range. In fact, it is very hard to emulate without having actually experienced it.

There is, however, a tremendous amount of progress to be made through systematic training and conditioning. One of the aspects of my training methodology that works so well is the mindset work that I base everything on. This is where fights are won. Everyone is so skill-focused or weapon-focused in this industry that it makes me wonder, who has actually done any up-close fighting? The point is that you can make arguably the largest advantage gains by building the orientation of what rests between your ears. Building the chassis to deliver that knowledge as force into the world only makes that better. Knowing what to do is always more powerful than having the capability to do things that you don't really know how to do.

Prison: The Orientation Training Camp

Everyone focuses on the thoughts of violence and rape when they talk about prison, because that is what Hollywood has made you believe. The real horror of prison is what is not often talked about: the intense and seemingly unending psychological trauma and conditioning prisoners are subjected to. No one cares about it, until you realize one day that these guys are then turned loose, and you will have to deal with them. Then, it's a big problem.

Prisons in the U.S. are not as bad as some third world countries, but they are still incredibly cruel places. They are designed to break you down to nothing, to less than human. A great amount of the guards devolve into cruelty because they dehumanize the prisoner, they feel absolute power over them. (This was absolutely showcased in the well-known Stanford Prison Experiment, where average people were put into the roles of prisoners and guards, and the "guards" actually became more and more cruel as the experiment went on.) The security procedures strip away any and all privacy, to the point of making you strip down naked in front of guards and other prisoners, bend over and spread your butt cheeks, and sometimes being made to low crawl across the dirty floor naked. You will be locked in a cage, spoken to and treated like a worthless animal that no one even wants to be alive, and deprived of all affectionate or compassionate human contact for years on end. The lights never, ever get turned off. You are surrounded by fluorescent lighting 24 hours a day. Add to this the ever-present threat of violence and sexual aggression, the horrible food, terrible sleeping conditions, bugs, roaches, rats, mice...you get the point, right?

Everything I described to you, I experienced firsthand. There is video evidence of this available out there as well, the HBO special "Gladiator Days" being one example. The reason it's important to know this is because the person you face may have been mentally trained in this way. Although the system is designed to break people, it largely fails and instead creates intensely hard human beings who can shut down their attachments on demand and actually hate you for no personal reason of your own doing. I mean, it sure as hell didn't break me. And just because I appear educated and articulate doesn't mean that I did not get the full training experience from a program that creates the mentally hardest motherfuckers in the U.S. Just imagine how bad it is when the person does not have a moral compass that values human life.

What is an effective "combat mindset"?

As I have stated for quite some time in my classes, articles and videos, an effective combat or fighting mindset is simply a mindset of extreme self-control under all conditions. While the cool factor of *"always being ready for the fight!"* can be appealing and looks good on a t-shirt, the truth is that you can be completely ready to fight and also completely out of control. This is not advisable if your goal is to have every advantage in the fight as possible. The ability to make good decisions under pressure, and then to follow through on those decisions with good action while adjusting to the fluid, changing circumstances of a fight is truly what gets you to victory. *But what does this actually mean?* How do we reach that level of mindset?

Developing your orientation is a process

The development of your orientation to violence is a process. Your orientation is the foundation by which all of your decisions are made. It is the culmination of your experiences, your cultural beliefs, your attachments and your confidence with arms. Developing an orientation to violence is a process. The process happens more quickly for those who have experience operating in dangerous environments for prolonged periods of time at a certain stress level. That usually brings along with it life altering events that violently shift your paradigm. It also brings with it a growing level of confidence in one's abilities to respond and deal with adverse conditions. This is as equally true for the criminal and their environments of gang neighborhoods, domestic violence and prison as it is for the soldier and their war zone operations.

At worst, for most, you may only have one confrontation in your life. Therefore, listening to people who have had many confrontations is an important part of preparing for that one. There are many verticals--LE, military, criminal underworld--that put people in a position to have to perform it, deal with the aftermath, live with it, and be ready to roll out and do it all over again the next day. (Having experienced it does not necessarily mean you can teach others about it, but I do believe it is one requirement to be able to articulate it properly.)

An often-overlooked part of orientation development is that many people cannot deal with serious, paradigm-shifting confrontation well. That problem is rooted in the components of your Orientation: your cultural, religious, genetics, moral and ethical beliefs, along with your dependence upon attachments and your confidence (or lack thereof) in your capabilities. How you deal with the aftermath may have the greatest impact on your orientation toward the next event you face. This is why I stress so heavily that in order to be victorious you must be able to win the physical fight, be cleared of criminal charges, be cleared of civil charges, not be ostracized socially, and come out psychologically healthy. Losing any one of those components of a fight can irreparably damage your orientation for the future. I know, I have lost in more than one of them.

Orientation and its effect on fighting capability

Two things happen in an orientation cycle: the application of your pre-existing paradigm to the problem at hand, and the synthesis of new information coming in real-time. It is the filter through which all things are observed, and all decisions are made. The speed with which we go from observance to decision to action is determined by factors we can change, and factors we cannot change, as well.

I believe that it is true that you cannot "speed up your brain". One of the best explanations I have ever heard was during a lecture from John Chapman where he stated, basically, that we are born with whatever processor speed we have, and we can't change that. What we can do, is limit what we allow to use our processor resources up. So, by training basic fundamental skills to a nearly automatic level, we free up our processor to be able to take in information and make decisions quicker and more thoroughly.

This was during an EAG Shoothouse course and it made perfect sense by days 3 and 4, as the shooters began to have the basics of *breach, dig corner, collapse sector* down to a science, allowing for brain power to be used on observation and processing new information--critical elements for success in hostile CQB environments. At that point, not having to use processor speed on basic skills allowed the students to begin to flow through problems seamlessly with better times and less mistakes. By eliminating the unnecessary thoughts, images and patterns from using your processor resources, you are clearer to focus on synthesizing the new information coming in and free to act upon it.

The other part of this equation is confidence. Having confidence in one's skill set, the fighter is able to choose the proper response to the threat *and follow through without hesitation*. By not clogging your brain's resources with fundamental skills and decisions, and also by having an earned confidence in your skills, the result is that the fighter can maintain a constant effort of menacing the opponent with enough effective violence to constantly derail the opponent's own orientation to the situation. This will cause confusion, uncertainty, paralysis and eventually defeat.

One issue I've run into when attempting to explain this concept is that people often mistake experience for orientation. You'll hear phrases like, "Yes, that's what we mean when we say experience is what you get right after you need it." No, orientation is not created solely by experience of doing it. Orientation, your worldview and decision-making capabilities, is a conditioned paradigm made up of many components. Conditioning and experience equally build your orientation, but adjustments must be made to culture, values and attachments as well.

Defeat his mind

Victory: Utilize Self-knowledge to Win

Sun Tzu clearly was a fan of disrupting the enemy mentally with any means necessary. *The Art of War* is all about using deception, strength, speed and constant pressure to literally shape the enemy's perception of the world coming at him. Col John Boyd wrote extensively about the importance of uncertainty, both in eliminating it in your perception (denying those negative mental patterns), and in creating it for your opponent. Uncertainty is the cradle of fear, anxiety and doubt. This is arguably the most important and fascinating aspect of fighting: attacking your opponent in his mind.

When we have reconciled our own orientation to violence through mission clarity, rules of engagement, moral application, the proper training of fundamental skills to the unconscious competent level, and most of all have denied the negative images of defeat from entering our minds, we have gained an extremely valuable insight into how the mind works. Your opponent's mind works in very similar ways, regardless of his mission difference from your own. By defeating yourself, you have gained the insight necessary to defeat your opponent. What was difficult for you to overcome, mainly uncertainty, is also his most difficult enemy. By applying violence of action and overwhelming force, or at least repeatedly denying your opponent from achieving his planned goals, you begin to cultivate the perception of uncertainty in his mind.

THIS is the essence of getting inside of his confidence. Literally changing the opponent's orientation to the situation at hand to the effect of growing uncertainty. There is no way in this book to discuss the endless sub-topics of fighting, violence and fight psychology. In fact, it's a struggle to truncate this information while not getting too technical, to keep this at the introductory level. However, it is important to note that within the above laid information rests all of the concepts from striking for your opponent's vulnerabilities, and making your weaknesses become strengths, all the way to dealing with the aftermath of a confrontation and surviving the legal, social, and psychological effects of deadly conflict. There simply is so much more to training than going to the range and learning how to shoot; or going to the dojo and learning some hand-to-hand technique.

My primary goal in fight training is to simply train people to fight, with firearms and without. Teaching shooting is easy, and somewhat boring. **Fighting, however, is complex and takes years to cultivate.** Especially if you lack that experiential shift of orientation. Which makes this task much more difficult in terms of teaching fighters. This is why I work overtime to expose as many of you as I can to the deeper thought processes that are involved on the other side of that paradigm shift. Most people do not have the attention span or frame of reference for the long haul of learning and self-development in fighting to a professional level. They come out for one or two shooting classes and think they are good to go. This is the definition of "you don't know what you don't know". It's very difficult to cultivate the thought process that is necessary for a non-fighter to realize that there is a vast of world of training that exists solely within the mind. Especially with the American Way of commercializing the "cool" stuff: technique, gear and lots of BANG action in the gym and on the range.

The big reward comes when the students who have never been in a confrontation recognize the genuine quality of the information provided by those who have. This enables them to realize that there is a big world inside the topic of violence, and no one has all of the answers. But the answers simply don't come

176

from people, who have never really been there, hypothesizing about how it all works. When they recognize those limitations within themselves, they begin to recognize them in sources of information about the subject, they choose instructors more wisely and learning occurs.

Take these concepts and roll them around in your head until you wake up one day and it's there. The light will break through. Don't let anything get your heart rate up, no matter how bad it looks. With a clearly established mission, legal boundaries, threat assessment, and repetitive training, eventually you can roll through the problem and just look for work. You will know what you can and cannot do. You will also know what eats at the mind of your opponent, because you defeated what ate at your own confidence. Why the Violent Criminal is better at it than you.

Where most "good guys" would be at a major disadvantage against the "bad guy" is: MINDSET. While it's safe to say that the majority of CCW license holders and police officers are decent people who were raised to believe violence was something to avoid and typically hope they never have to use deadly force on another human being, *the bad guy is quite likely the opposite.* They do not have the reservations about violence that non-criminally minded people do. They most often have grown up in environments where violence was actually glorified. In many homes and communities—like the one I grew up in—violence is tied directly to deep developmental concepts like self-worth, social rank, and "manhood." A violent home, the hard street life, gang or thug culture, physical and emotional abuse as a child; whatever the reason, you can bet they *do not* have the same aversion to actual violence that you do and THEY ARE PROBABLY MORE EXPERIENCED AT IT THAN YOU ARE. They may also have a healthy dose of projected hate for you that will assist their decision in eliminating you to get what they want.

This is a street version of the combat mindset, *and it can be hardcore and ruthless when mixed with the experience and hatred of a criminal mind.* Understanding these facts about the lack of preparation that just owning a gun or having a qualification gives you and the seriousness of the threats you may face out there; it is imperative that you be willing to train just a little bit harder and smarter.

Good training will subject you to some induced stress, to prepare you as much as possible, for that potentially fatal event. But all training cannot just focus on shooting or fighting skills. I often say in classes, you can be the fastest, most accurate and flashiest shooter on the range and it will all mean ZERO if you are frozen in fear or fumbling in a panic during a life or death situation. You must re-orient yourself to violence. You must train the mind above all else. That is what life has done for your enemy.

When your life is threatened, and *all of the legal criteria for justified lethal force have been met*, then speed, efficiency and ruthlessness better be all that are on your mind. The only way to clear your mind of everything else and be able to focus on your job is to train yourself to that automatic level, both mentally and physically, and to fully believe in what you are doing without any doubts whatsoever. Like your attacker, your willingness to follow through must be clearly worked out well before any encounter takes place. This includes knowing what you are allowed to do to stay out of prison. I hammer this point home in my classes when we talk about decisiveness and mindset. The decision must be made long before the moment comes, and the parameters must be clearly defined and adhered to.

Competency increases confidence, and confidence reduces the effects of fear. Fear is the number one stimulus that releases the panic cocktail into the bloodstream and triggers negative effects such as skyrocketing heart rate, reduced vision and hearing and a loss of rational thought. Remember, fear is largely perceptual. One person may be extremely joyful while jumping out of an airplane, thousands of feet above the earth, while I personally would be sent into a terrible panic. Jumping out of the plane is not different from one person to the other, but their perception of it is. It is a lack of confidence (and the uncertainty that results) that contributes most to the fear of the unknown.

If you are preoccupied with what might happen to you (fear), you will not be focused on making things happen to live (open your chute). It's very simple; build your confidence in your skills and you will be able to focus on getting that job done. Building skill sets and thoroughly testing those skill sets is how you build the confidence that begins to shift your perception of problems that replaces uncertainty with certainty.

The two components of a deadly force confrontation that are most important are: fundamental fighting skills and mindset. While being able to draw a weapon quickly and land positive hits on target is crucial, it is mindset that will get you through in the end. If you cannot maintain your level of fighting skills and procedural training under high-stress and make life-or-death decisions in a hyper-fast, changing situation, you can and will make fatal mistakes.

While I'm primarily referencing those confrontations where violence is imminent, I can't talk about the subject without mentioning that is also "mindset" that will help you to avoid 90% of violent encounters altogether. There is so much more to having a proper self-defense mindset than just being willing to fight through a deadly encounter. How we see ourselves, how well we maintain our awareness at all times, where we choose to go and who we choose to be around, how well we control our ego, how we handle minor conflicts and disagreements…all of this, and more, are huge components of maintaining a proper self-defense mindset. Knowing when NOT to engage, as well as knowing when to STOP engaging, are just as important as being willing and able to engage in physical combat. There are very strict rules of engagement in our society for dealing with violence. Entering into a conflict without the proper mindset will make it very difficult for you to avoid crossing a line and ruining your life.

When it comes down to an actual violent attack on you or your loved ones it's important to understand the mindset you will be up against. Take a good, hard look at the level of criminal animal that is out there. They have less fear than you. They have more violence in their veins than you do. They have more battle scars than you have. They may be sociopathic, psychopathic, or simply have their entire ego invested in their "street cred" (which they will add to by victimizing or eliminating you.) Trust me, less of you are ready to hit that head-on than you think. Don't ever discount the viciousness and efficiency of your attacker's mindset. Even if you are a decent shooter/fighter and have done some stress-inducing drills, shooting/fighting skill are only a small component of winning a fight. Mindset is what truly brings you home at the end of the day. Especially when going up against someone who is used to doing the real deal.

Preparing for Orientation

(This appeared in an interview that Conflict Manager Magazine did with me in 2017)

It amazes me, having participated in and committed a considerable amount of extreme violence, that trainers and other "experts" literally skip over real orientation work and focus solely on technique and skill. I find reality to be quite the opposite and I will give the fight bet to the guy with no technique but who has a highly developed orientation to violence over the guy with great technique but no orientation to violence. Every time. I've WATCHED it happen. I've BEEN the guy with no technique against trained arts. So, I started using the term "Violence of Mind". There can be no effective violence of action without violence of mind.

It's very important to emphasize the critical nature of the blocking of negative mental images that we discussed. Every great martial strategist from Miyamoto Musashi, to Sun Tzu, to Col. John Boyd have all said this. I have a saying that I teach my students,

"Your opponent's mind works in very similar ways to your own. By defeating yourself, you have gained the insight necessary to defeat your opponent. What was difficult for you to overcome-- mainly uncertainty--is also his most difficult enemy."

So the fighter that truly understands himself or herself, who has honest self-awareness, and like naturally occurring technique they develop naturally occurring confidence, can begin to understand their opponent in a way that few will ever see. This is the framework of that "feel" I speak of, which some refer to as *non-conscious processing*. Just like the technique that naturally arises from hard work and adaptation of the raw principles, there is a subconscious confidence that arises from hard work and experience that will naturally block the negative thought patterns, and also seeks to cause the negative thought patterns in the enemy. There are two results of this that are desirable: solidifying your own confidence, and the ability to break your opponent's confidence.

This is what Musashi refers to when he talks about mastering perception and "causing confusion by acting so that your opponent's mind becomes uncertain" and "sends his mind in different directions, making him think various things, and having him wonder if you will be slow or quick." It wasn't just Musashi. Sun Tzu said, "Warfare is the Tao of deception." Of course, that deception was, by his descriptions, nearly always designed to gain the violence of action surprise, or wear the enemy down, for the express purpose to create enough uncertainty in the enemy's mind to defeat him. This is why orientation, self-control and the art of concealment are more important than any other skills in the long term.

For so many to have read these words from these great violence analysts but give little thought to developing the orientation that allows these things to happen is perplexing to me. Boyd referred to Orientation as the "schwerpunkt", the main focus, the most important. And it is. Few have seen the level and volume of domestic violence that I have and go on to be articulate about it. If they are out there, their voices are not being heard. What we have instead are a bunch of experts that are either trainees who have had little actual exposure to serious murder violence, or guys who have been uniformed by the government and given a supply chain, back up, a brotherhood, radios, and a disparity of force in almost all confrontations that is on their side. Neither of these will create that orientation needed to adapt to street level murderous violence one person can bring to you by surprise.

For example, I have noticed many times how differently I perceive violence and its possible effects when compared to many of the professionals I have known. Ex-soldiers, SWAT cops, sport fighters...many of them seem to measure violence ability exclusively by things like strength, marksmanship, technique, or mat experience. To me, none of these things are measures of *violence ability*. They are measures of things that can ASSIST with violence ability.

Violence ability also is not just the willingness to do violence either. I have come to believe over the years that true violence is something that lives in your heart, meaning it is deeply rooted in your orientation. It's the difference between just thinking about fighting and beating a man in a show of force that is somewhat of a contest, compared to thinking about ambushing a man with a knife and delivering as many short, rapid strokes deep into his motherfucking neck as quickly as you can, *because FUCK HIM that's why.*

THIS is the level of violence that I have known, not only in prison but also growing up and even in my childhood home. This is violence that must come from the heart, it is totally void of any bluffing. It thirsts to destroy completely and thoroughly and does not need any sense of fairness to feel justified. It is very dark, and only comes from conditioning and orientation that are starkly different than what you receive in training.

So, now you have to think about the deeper more esoteric developments of naturally occurring technique and confidence and realize that these do not just develop from wholesome training. I know guys who have been shooting, stabbing and shanking people for decades and they are amazingly effective fighters, but have very little education or training. And this is a guy who you will look at and think, "I'll beat the shit out of him" or "I'll submit him quickly", but in reality, while you may be more skillful than he is, he is much quicker and severely more oriented toward murdering you quickly and violently than you ever will be toward him. It's just how it is. This is the difference between talking about sport fighting, or even bar brawling, compared to going up against a seriously violent person.

To bring it full circle, there are many killers out there who have achieved that "no mind" level of ability in fighting without discipline and training. There was a time period in my life when I operated completely without rules. There are always rules in a fight, but only IF you care about those rules. But for someone that doesn't care about laws, consequences and even has no fear of death and no attachments on earth, operating without rules is pretty easy.

The point I am driving at is that the things which we must defeat to achieve naturally occurring confidence, technique and no-mind flow are mainly the negative images and thought patterns associated with our uncertainties (lack of confidence) and our attachments, which are affected by both our fear of losing our lives/freedom and losing people we care about. The really bad guy has transcended those fears and attachments easily by removing the root causes of them altogether. I hated my life as a kid, and always said, "I didn't ask to be born into this fucking shit" so I legitimately kind of wanted to die, in a blaze of glory would have made it all the better! There are others out there who operate like that lifelong. Their orientation is one you cannot even begin to understand.

The closest the student can come to this is to be guided into as much naturally occurring confidence and technique as possible, while also being guided in a serious orientation toward violence. Because that is truly a source of rock solid confidence and capabilities. This comes through conditioning and guidance from experience. Training should go after the root causes of adverse habits and traits. For example, don't train to get better under stress as much as you should train to just not react with stress period. Don't train to build confidence without addressing the causes of uncertainties, which is a combination of lack of

183

confidence and your attachments to life, liberty, loved ones, etc. You cannot develop by staying shallow. In all things in life, self-awareness is the first path to success.

Criminal Combat Culture

The reason that the gunfight training industry is such a self-policing industry is because we have a great number of participants who have actually been in gunfights and real fights. Between a dozen or more years in the war on terror, and high level police work, and the few rare crossover guys like me, there are a number of teachers who are teaching from real experience. With so much real experience in a field, it's hard to push bullshit and get away with it, and it's getting even harder. This is a good thing. The martial arts self-defense industry does not have that. No other martial group can boast the same amount of experience within its ranks.

When it comes to criminal violence, no one knows it better than the violent criminals. They also live within a system of violence education that is self-policing with something even more powerful: natural selection. Their system has evolved. They have grown with it. Violent culture has emerged differently each generation and, through the close cultural controls of neighborhoods and prison, it has been very condensed and largely self-contained. What this has produced is a pure, uncontaminated strain of violence mindset than previously encountered. At its purest it is itself a warrior culture passed down for generations. They study the same masters, and read Tzu, Musashi, and others. They refine and employ tactics. They teach one another.

It has been said by others that humans are essentially animals that learn by playing. This is why sparring and rolling work so well to *introduce* us to combat. But this only works to a certain, limited, extent. What works better than anything is to *learn by doing*. We can be taught, read about, watch and pretend to do a task, but until we actually do it we do not really know it. This is where criminal combat culture becomes really effective. Through rough and splintered families, bad neighborhoods and schools, and ultimately prison, a self-policing system of conditioning takes place that involves a very high amount of actual violence. It begins at a very early age with beatings and mistreatment, and spills out into the streets with fights from early grade school on. Those who land in prison reach the highest levels of training and experience, both mentally and physically.

In the beginning, as young children, the anger and toughness are often already there. Their strength and full commitment sometimes have not caught up yet, but it does so very quickly. It's very difficult to understand if you have not come from this world. Even those who have studied and worked closely with criminals, there are things you just cannot "get". You can hear the stories about the beatings, the drug use, but you will never *feel* the crack in a person's paradigm when the ones they love and look up to become unpredictable, violent, hurtful, and then they die. You can listen, and try to empathize, but you can never see the world through the eyes that have felt that. You can't. That is why you should listen. Listen to those who have, and do, see the world through those eyes.

As I mentioned before, violence was glorified in my family growing up. Just like it is in most ghettos and broken families shattered by drugs and alcohol and prison sentences. As a small child, searching for praise and recognition, my young ears heard the enthusiasm that the family spoke with when they talked about all of the violent things my family members had done. This leaves you walking away thinking, "I'm going to fuck shit up ten times better than any of them. I want that praise and more!" It's a ranking system on the streets, in the neighborhood, in the school. It's a ranking system in the family in some cases (like mine was).

Even families that don't think they are advocating it; do not realize the damage they are doing when they tell the enthusiastic stories of violence. Their lack of common sense and education, mixed with altered/diminished cognitive abilities due to years of

185

drug and alcohol use, doesn't allow them to understand the consequences of their actions.

The world that the violent criminal grows up in is often a harsh one. It's a world where society already looks down on you the day you are born, where you can't make friends at school with anyone from a decent family because they are forbidden to talk to you (because you'll be a bad influence, introduce their child to drugs, steal from them, and whatever else their square minds can conjure up). And it's not just limited to certain races as some ridiculously seem to believe, I'm white and I never had a choice where or how I grew up.

You are born second class. This is a version of what is meant by "the sins of the father..." You will pay dearly for the mistakes of your elders in your family. I remember going to school and having to listen to stories in class, in front of all of the other kids, about how bad my uncles and aunts were. I was from that family where the cops were always showing up to arrest someone, or someone was always going to prison or dying in a fight or a drug overdose. You don't stand a fucking chance. You have no social power. *Except violence.*

At the bottom, violence is the one fucking thing you have that no one can take away. It's the one thing that most people in society do not have, so you have some real power now. Their social power, their bureaucratic authority, all are powerless to real violence. When you apply it with anger, hatred, apathy or revenge, then it becomes extremely powerful and most often an ambush game. Either way, it very often is the only taste of being something other than a second-class person that someone from those demographics will experience. When you give someone a taste of power, after they have been mistreated their entire life, very often the results are just bad.

I'll share a personal story of restraint here. Growing up, and of course all through prison, violence was a viable and often used answer for power. After my release, I was demoted to a financially poor ex-convict with no power at all. I retired my violent ways because I didn't want to live in prison or die, so I couldn't just fuck people up when they challenged me anymore. I had enough of that *wasting my in-life prison* shit. So, a few years after my release, I found myself married with a beautiful new daughter, working hard in the dirty auto body business, and trying my best to do it the right way. We constantly fell on hard times and no matter how hard I worked, we had to move around and put stuff in storage units.

This particular time we had some items in a storage unit, and we went to get our stuff out of it to move into another place. We owed about $35 on the unit at that time but *we weren't past due*. I planned on sending the payment in at the normal time just like any other month. While we were unloading, the owner of the units showed up. A cocky and downright mean man who had obviously been skipped out on enough to look at anyone moving out like a thief. He rolls up on us and begins talking to my (at that time) wife. I finished loading something and I walked up to them to see what was going on. That is when it happened. Murder flowed through my veins.

He looked at me approaching with fire-hot disdain and hatred in his eyes. I mean this man was sending me a clear message of "don't fuck with me today," and this was confirmed with the tone of the shit he talked to me afterwards about *his money*. My insides burned with the heat of a thousand hells filled with hatred to the fucking brim of each one. I wanted to stomp his fucking guts out and cave his face in until I was physically exhausted. Maybe I would take a break, eat a sandwich, and cave his face in some fucking more. Maybe I would stab him in the neck while I got drunk on the terror pouring out of his eyes. He would have been dragged into a world he was not ready for. He had no idea. He was a wealthy guy, not terribly physically strong looking, and had the *feeling* of the good life.

I, on the other hand, had seen the light go out of men's eyes after proclaiming their power over another. I had watched the look in men's eyes, just like his, when they look up from the ground terrified and begging for their life, mumbling some shit about their families and not wanting to die. And because I had tasted that, my mouth watered uncontrollably when it was so near again. To take someone who thinks they can just treat you any way they want, thinks they can rule over you, abuse you, spit on you...to look them directly in their scared and surprised eyes while blood squirts out of the knife wounds in their neck is pure power. They always get this surprised look in their eyes, like they never thought it would happen to them. But it did.

I let him live that day, and every day he's lived since then is a gift from me. He wasn't the only one in those first 5 or 6 years. There's a few of you motherfuckers out there that have no idea how lucky you really are. Of course, I succeeded in beating those urges and now, after 20 plus years, my family and my professionalism are unquestionably more important than teaching some shithead a lesson about real power. But how many guys didn't overcome that? How many are out there as a ticking bomb looking for a trip wire? More than you'll ever know.

You need to have a basic understanding of what creates that orientation to violence because, in some ways, you are going to have to simulate this process inside of your own mind. You can never duplicate the hardening process that a violent criminal has went through to get to the orientation level that he is at. Just make sure that you do not overestimate your own capabilities while projecting stupidity onto him by underestimating how violent he is. You just got a small glimpse into that mind, be sure to think about that the next time you issue a challenge, especially to someone is who socially *lower* than you.

"The most dangerous creation of any society is the man who has nothing to lose." - James A. Baldwin

The fatal mistakes of underestimation

One of the points I try to drive home in this business is respecting the experience and dangerousness of the violent criminal fighter. I've heard so much talk of how stupid and ineffective criminals are, and just derogatory talk downward about the violent criminal in general. There's even a persistent attitude out there that "professionals" are the only dangerous people, and civilians don't know anything about "fighting." That is flat out wrong. If civilians didn't know anything about fighting, why do you need SWAT teams, tons of equipment, and heavy training to go out and face...civilians? Why are "civilians" doing all of the killing on our streets? I remember once in a back-alley bar in Cleveland getting dragged into, and quickly getting out of, a ridiculous, drunken argument with a former Ranger and Blackwater contractor about who is "better for the job" of criminal assassin. I did not and would never initiate or willingly enter into such a stupid discussion, but I was dragged into it long enough to hear the Ranger get aggravated and talk about how there are "much better people for the job" than any civilian

I squashed the argument by changing the subject and not even engaging it. However, it revealed to me that superiority complex held by the Ranger, and many other "professionals" like him. And this is why they are wrong. Civilians are the ones doing all of the killing out here. When they catch the rare hitman, he is most often a ruthless criminal raised up in South America, or Eastern Europe, and has been a criminal his whole life. The irony of the situation is that the Ranger in that argument never shot another human in service. Nor will he most likely ever. He also did not grow up in or ever operate near the criminal element in the U.S. Yet he can tell you all about who is the most dangerous people in the continental U.S....

When you look at most *high-level* professionals, with the exception of a few, they come from stellar sports, academic and family backgrounds. They excelled their whole life by following rules and performing as expected. You cannot become a high-level operator in the U.S. military or special operations law enforcement with a bad record, poor performance and criminal experience. So just keep in mind, while you were getting decent grades, playing football and going to wrestling state championships with your family cheering you on, your criminal counterpart was out there banging, cracking skulls and shooting people, all while feeling like the world didn't want him to fucking begin with. We were carrying weapons around our neighborhoods by the time we were 12 or 13. You have to look at the difference in conditioning and orientation that this creates.

I guarantee if you walked the streets of certain Chicago neighborhoods you would encounter "fighters" who have a shit ton more experience and drive for blood than you'll ever have, just based on the orientation and amount of bloodletting they have done. The same was true in the late 1980's and early 1990's in most cities, including my hometown of Youngstown. My own experience put me directly with the worst of the worst criminals from one of the worst violent crime eras we've had. And I'm not even touching on the influx of cartel experienced criminals flowing in with the drug and human trafficking trades.

Does this equate to "skills"? Yes, it does. Yet, people will still disagree with this because their ego just won't let them say something they perceive as being "positive" about a criminal. Stop looking for things and start looking at them. Skills are neither positive nor negative, they just are. How they are applied is what matters. The criminal that has grown up fighting, stabbing, shooting, stealing, concealing, etc. has most definitely developed skills. Skills that you cannot get in your gym or on your range.

You have to take into consideration the perspective that I am speaking from. Try to understand that I was pushed into a world that collected criminals in one place. That means all of the really bad ones, in one place. If you are a patrol cop, you might run into a really bad one once or twice, unless you're working a bad metro area. But you will never eat breakfast, lunch and dinner with him, or sleep in the same room as him. Honestly, most people will never have an encounter with the truly bad criminal. So, there is a normalcy bias that prohibits you from initially understanding how I could have daily contact with numerous hyper-violent criminals for years on end. Not only was I raised by hyper-violent people, I ended up locked up with killers and extremely criminally violent people where I had to live with them, eat with them, sleep in the same room as them, play cards with them, and, fight them. I was one of them. I may have had a slightly

190

different moral code concerning innocent people (I have never victimized innocent people), but I was without a doubt one of the wolves in that den.

While it is true that a good majority of criminals you will encounter are mostly low-level assholes that can't fight, you are free to mistake that as a representation of every possible encounter at your own peril. There are seriously deadly people out there, many with more CONUS kills than you'll ever have. You may have to face him one day. And guess what? It's his turf. You have rules and he doesn't. You may think they are not that plentiful because you don't run in those circles. I personally have known dozens of them.

Target Analysis vs. Target Selection

One of the biggest myths of the self-defense industry is that looking like a hard target will keep you from being selected as a target. Think about this for a moment. Consider all of the things that I've talked about so far, the hatred, the power struggle, all of it. Consider that prisons are full of "hard targets" and yet they get attacked and die every day in this country's prison system. If being jacked up and being aware truly deterred criminal violence, the violence in our prison system would be nearly non-existent. The weak ones submit quickly. Violence only really needs to be utilized against the harder targets. This is why I teach the reality of *target analysis* over target selection. A real predator will analyze a target and approach accordingly. Remember, he has the ultimate advantage that you do not know he is coming. Target selection has more to do with reason, opportunity and resource need than it does with how much force will be needed to take the target down. ANY target can be taken down if caught unaware. And we are all unaware multiple times throughout our days.

There are countless interviews available in full video format online of hardened killers detailing how they analyze a target. They outline things like: Does he look fit or strong? Does he appear mentally sharp? Who are his friends and is he alone

191

much? Etc. This is very common in prison and criminal combat culture. I myself will look at several key features automatically if I perceive someone to be a potential opponent. Strength, size, posture, structure, path of movement, footwear, clothing type...all of these can be both signs of weaknesses or vulnerabilities in how that person could fight.

The other side of it is projected confidence. Too much of it and it becomes a liability to you because the predator reads that as both an insult because you think you are tough or something, and as an opportunity to strike because overconfidence typically breeds underestimation of your opponent. So this is a rather complex system of cues that are used not so much to select targets, but more so to analyze how to take the target down. The arts of concealment and ambush trump your "hard to kill" skills.

Now, don't get me wrong. I am in no way saying that you should not have advantages on your side. And, of course, I wouldn't be telling you to appear weak. What I am introducing is the idea that just because you are aware and look tough is not ever a guarantee that you will not be selected. To believe that is just a logical fallacy.

CHAPTER ELEVEN: CONCEALMENT: MORE THAN JUST HIDING A GUN

"We serial killers are your sons, we are your husbands, we are everywhere. And there will be more of your children dead tomorrow…
Society wants to believe it can identify evil people, or bad or harmful people, but it's not practical. There are no stereotypes."

-Ted Bundy, serial killer who tortured and murdered over thirty women

Ted Bundy was described as charming and good looking. But that was not his true power, the thing that made him one of the deadliest men that lived in modern times. Ted used a baiting technique of typically dressing like a victim of injury: crutches, arm slings, or otherwise injured to gain the trust of unsuspecting women through pity or empathy. While we can certainly argue that what sets men like him apart is the ability to kill in a way that others just cannot fathom, we cannot deny that the very thing that made him so effective a predator was: concealment. Bundy concealed his weapons, his intentions, his capabilities, his darkness. He concealed his evil. So, we can identify his primary dangerousness as a predator as a perfection of the art of concealment.

Why do I use this despicable human being as an example? Because he is the poster boy of what the enemy can accomplish with concealment. Over 30 kills. Before you understand how important concealment is to your own training and daily life, you should clearly understand how vital it is to your enemy. The criminal element has been practicing concealment way longer than you have, and for higher stakes. They were hiding drugs, weapons, lies and other intentions from their families, school officials, police and society in many cases for their entire lives.

And here you are, thinking "concealment" means not printing with a pistol under your shirt.

In the natural world, there are very few predators that, while operating in predator mode, allow themselves to be seen early in the stalk. Predators and ambush go hand-in-hand, but ambush does not always mean blindsided. Often, it's simply positioning to a more advantageous position. Human predators operate exactly the same way. It's actually much easier to get close to us, because we have social norms and boundaries that leave us vulnerable. If someone approaches you on the street in a seemingly non-threatening way, it is simply unacceptable to flail your arms about, yell wildly and brandish a weapon on them. This is what I refer to as *the exploitation of social courtesies*. The criminal predator knows how to get close to you, often times within touching distance, before you can reasonably set a boundary. Therefore, the art of concealment becomes your attackers, and your, greatest asset.

The work now begins to make concealment *your* greatest asset. By understanding how it works, to be a predator yourself, you can begin to cultivate an attitude of concealment that becomes a daily practice. This need not be deceptive in a negative way. Your moral code and sense of protectiveness can lead your decisions. But you do need to understand concealment and positioning if you want to win in a predator vs predator situation.

Concealment is an ultimate advantage, all day long. You have knowledge that no one knows you have. You have skills that no one knows you have. You have capabilities that no one knows you have. You have essentially adapted to the laws of the jungle, and can meet the predator at his own game.

Operator clothes will get you kilt in da streets!

Will wearing certain clothing, like gun company hats and tactical pants, get you targeted first? Maybe. Is there evidence of

194

this? Yes. Not specifically civilians in tactical pants, but in today's world police officers are targeted for attack and ambush style assassination very frequently in the U.S. While it is only reaching our consciousness in this country, this is actually an epidemic problem in third world countries.

The number one indicator used to identify the officer is the uniform. Very often in robberies the sleepy, elderly uniformed security guard is the first to go down as well. These are very well-known facts. So, yes. There is evidence that clothing choice can be an indicator to target you. Gang colors, uniforms, "tourist" apparel in third world countries or rough cities, the list goes on. Every one of them with heavily documented cases to back up the claim that clothing can identify you as a threat or a target of opportunity. Either conclusion in the bad guy's mind is bad news for you, news that you will receive last.

One thing I can say, from very extensive experience in the criminal predator world, is that clothing is not a final indicator, ever. For example, I see through the eyes of a predator. I have hated before. I have hunted other predators in hostile environments. Very often when I am out, especially on days when the gun show is in town, I will see someone dressed in the *deterrent uniform* of tactical pants, printing pistol, maybe even open carrying, etc. Many of these times I can sense that there are no real teeth behind that bark. What I mean is as a predator that has engaged in close combat with many, many different human beings, you get a real sense of capabilities from a number of cues. Posture, physical fitness, size, apparent strength or weakness, a look in the eyes, demeanor, confidence in small movements (large ones are easy to fake), stance, how the feet move, how the weight is shifted, etc. all tell me what to expect and where to attack if needed.

One conclusion is if you are not physically strong, confident and great at fighting, you better practice full concealment really well, because you cannot overcome the indicative cues you are throwing off. Your best hope is a strong counter-ambush, and you better be really damn good at it. That's

195

straight from the mouth of the wolf. Even if you are decked out in the most up-to-date tactical gear and have the meanest look on your face, we can tell if you are really just a *buster ass mark*. Get over yourselves and live as something real.

Openly carrying gives away nearly all of your advantage. I won't even argue that here. I am just going to talk about concealment, and say that it is everything that open carry is not. I am not interested in using a gun as a political statement. Nor am I interested in anyone's particular views about patriotism and desensitizing the public to firearms. The internet is full of arguments about how there's no proof that people are targeted for open carry, or how there's proof it's a deterrent. Go argue it there, I'm just not interested. Or better yet, use your open carry in a force-on-force class where they do robbery scenarios, and tell me how that works out when the unknown actor/robber ambushes you and suddenly you have two guns in your life: the bad guy's gun in your face, and your gun still in its holster. Usually if someone even comes with the open carry comments on social media, I act like they're not even commenting. In fact, this paragraph is already more than I want to give to that subject.

The question I cannot answer is, "why would you?" Why would you want to dress this way anyway? So, you can have more pockets? I just don't know. I've heard all of the arguments about deterrence, comfort, political statement. I still have yet to hear one that makes sense from a personal security and quality of life standpoint. Pretty much all of the high-level uniformed professionals that I know would ditch the uniform and go concealed all day if they could.

FULL CONCEALMENT

I am going to talk about this from the perspective of the criminal world, the one you are trying to prepare against. I was a part of that world for a long time. More importantly, I was raised in that world. I am talking here about the rules of that world, the one you may have to fight in one day. In terms of being a predator, concealing the danger until the last split second is an art. A person cannot prepare for, nor react to, a threat that they do not yet know exists. Timing is the key to winning when the prey has the capability of fighting back. When the prey is themselves a predator, or inherently has the same capabilities, the stakes are much higher, and concealment and timing become the *high arts* of the experienced.

The belief that criminals target the weak exclusively is just a myth. Police and CCW citizens are targeted every day in this country. Tom Givens' study of almost 70 student involved shootings revealed that *every student who was armed and trained and carrying a loaded weapon won the conflict*. While that is truly a homogenous and small sample, do you think they were all easy marks? Did they all *appear* easy? Not likely. But they were all attacked nonetheless.

From the criminal standpoint, the prey's preparations, training, capabilities, fitness, and weapons do not matter as much as the criminal's ambush skills. All of those strengths you have can be overcome easily with a well-executed ambush. So, guess what? The easiest way to overcome them is to know about them beforehand. Imagine that. How many combat vet, highly experienced and uniformed officers have died in the line of duty responding to a simple domestic call?

A well-placed shot from concealment during approach is all it takes to put an end to all of those capabilities. The glory of battle may be stolen from you altogether. The most dedicated bad guy will drop you before you know you are in a fight. It literally happens all the time. The more you project about your intentions or capabilities, the more you present them with the ultimatum of taking you down decisively in ambush or facing loss themselves. What if your overt projections of strength deterred 10 low-level fights that you could have probably won, only to give the advantage to the one high-level attacker that takes you down for good? Think that's bullshit? If you could ask the numerous cops

197

who have been executed simply sitting in their marked cruisers and uniforms, what do you think they would say?

While uniformed police and military often do not have the choice of fully covert concealment, as a civilian you do. You have the golden opportunity to play by the exact same rules as the predator you seek to stop. Full concealment is the art of concealing intentions, capabilities and weapons. Operator fantasies: if there was such a thing as a "civilian operator", they would be highly unrecognizable as such. In spite of appearing physically fit, they may appear to have a relaxed demeanor. In spite of appearing confident, they may be friendly for the express purpose of blending in and not drawing attention. They would have very little cues outbound in terms of capabilities and weapons. They would be the *"surprise motherfucker!"* that comes out of the dark corner with a dedicated purpose, defined mission, trained skills, and solid decision making. Be *that* guy and win.

CONCEALMENT IN PRACTICE

Concealment and self-control go hand-in-hand. Concealing your feelings until a problem is worked out is part of being in control. When we get pissed at a spouse or co-worker, we know that it is best to cool off and think it over, or to work on the problem without uncontrolled emotion until a resolution is met. Part of that process is concealing our emotions until we get them under control.

So, this is part of concealment. The untrained and undisciplined will begin to immediately change their demeanor when they feel fear or anger. This is always a betrayal of yourself. Concealing your intentions and capabilities means maintaining this control *during* a confrontation as much as it means concealment *before* a confrontation. For those who have rolled in BJJ, if you telegraph your moves your opponent will counter and cut you off. Fighting is the same way no matter if it is verbal or physical, no matter whether weapons will be involved or not.

Advantages are the name of the game when your life is on the line. Giving away cues and projecting intentions or capabilities is to lose those advantages.

A practical application for concealment is to work hard at not showing the world what an awesome warrior you are. Some people don't have the option of fully doing this, like law enforcement, military personnel, instructors, etc. Even writing this book is a betrayal of my own intentions and capabilities. But we choose to do this for the betterment of society, to help others and give the good guys the advantages through our knowledge or protection. (Believe me, I'm not telling the bad guys anything they don't already know.) But know this, everything you write or post on social media creates a complete profile of what you carry, how you train, and what you may know.

If you, however, do not fall into any of these categories, no one ever has to know how awesome you are or what weapons you are carrying. Even if you do post on social media, when you are out in public you still have the full opportunity to practice concealment and no one in your presence will know anything about you and what you can do in a moment's notice.

Lack of concealment is an ego issue. It is bred into us to want the world to know we are an *alpha,* or to position for rank. It is thousands of years of DNA encoding for breeding rights and social hierarchy placement and/or dominance. It's a hard thing to overcome. Discipline is the mark of a highly trained fighter. Allowing oneself to be underestimated, or at least overlooked (which is really the goal), is a privilege we have in modern society. It won't hurt our ability to get a date, because we now have social skills to make up for that. It won't mean that we can't eat because surviving in society is not based upon the alpha eating first and the betas taking scraps. We can be nice, pleasant, helpful, quiet, and a multitude of other things that don't scream "I'm a killer alpha don't fuck with me and let me breed and eat ARRGGHH!!"

There's absolutely nothing wrong with being a tough guy. There are things that I simply cannot hide. There are times that deterrence is the name of the game. But the takeaway is that you have the *option* of using it when you need it. Just like when I visit a dear friend in Baltimore and we walk the streets in some of the less-safe areas. She makes note of (and thoroughly enjoys) the fact that she is not cat-called, and we are not approached for money, drugs or any other reason. I am certain my upbringing, capabilities and five years in prison contribute to whatever it is they are reading on me that determines their decision not to engage us. But it is not guaranteed. Very easily one day that could be challenged. Especially for me, since I am really not a big guy. Over playing it will guarantee that challenge will eventually come. When it does, it will most likely be a serious challenge. That is the inherent danger of projecting for deterrence, that if you are challenged it will be a different level. You better not be bluffing.

Quite simply, outside of a uniform requirement, clothing and demeanor are a choice you have to make. Choose wisely. My advice is that it is situation dependent based on a lot of variables from your mission to the culture and "rules" of the area you will be in. But to broadcast it all of the time just seems to be begging for some type of recognition in an artificial way.

If you really are *about that life*, people will see it. And if you aren't real, well, they'll see that too.

What do the "experts" know?

I know that there are academics and others who have enumerated systems of cues or have gleaned some insight from criminal interviews and interaction about how victims are chosen. Here's what I will say about that: While much of it seems to be common sense and true, none of it ever sounds like the conversations we had in prison, or in drug filled rooms of the ghetto houses we grew up in. Not even close. The bottom line is that no amount of exposure, interviews, studies or tests can make the "experts" one of *us*. I say "us" not because I am a criminal by any definition today, but because I am from that cloth and will never forget the things that I know. Things that, if you were not there, living the life and doing it, you can never, ever know.

Let's not forget that the criminal being interviewed is someone who is adept at deceit and manipulation. On top of this is the complication of interview myths such as nonverbal cues and nervousness being universal tells of lying. It's simply not true and has been disproven, clinically, by many professionals. Even the FBI guidelines for field agents clearly details this fact on their website. But I don't need any confirmation to personally know it's true, I've lied and been lied to enough to know that sometimes you can't tell what someone is thinking, especially if they don't want you to know. When someone says, "I am just a bad liar; it's all over my face if I'm lying" what they are really saying is that they have very little control over certain emotions that are tied to the topic being lied about or to the act of lying itself. Essentially, it's a lack of self-control.

Now, most people who say that are probably decent, honest people that don't lie because they don't want to. But, be clear about what people are telling you. They are not saying they do not lie because it's wrong or they don't want to, they are saying they lack the self-control to do it successfully. When dealing with the hardened criminal, or worse, sociopath, they can have an extremely high degree of self-control.

That self-control is what makes them dangerous and effective. They have effectively detached themselves from their attachments, from their fears of prison or death, from their connectedness to their families. They have compartmentalized those attachments away from the event of being tested (being questioned, interviewed, interrogated). This lessens the emotional impact at the moment and allows the emotions to be controlled or "shut off" to a certain extent. With controlled emotions, concealment and deception become much easier.

Psychologists will argue that this "control approach" is flawed because the physiological symptoms that accompany strong emotional feelings are often beyond conscious control. This is true, until you short-circuit that process and eliminate the strong emotional feeling at the root of it. This is easier to do than you

201

would believe, once one is able to compartmentalize or cessate the attachments that cause the strong emotions.

Strong minds can practice a self-conditioning process that will work in concert with external conditioning factors to create a very emotionally unreactive person, on-demand. This is apparent, when thought about deeply enough, because it is the essence of what I am talking about in the mindset and orientation sections of this book. Hacking that system to achieve a superior level of self-control no matter what is coming at you. Criminals can do it.

While there are some universal cues and patterns of victim targeting that apply in large swaths across the lower level criminal element, I am more concerned with the higher-order criminal. My final thought about it is this: beware of applying what the "experts" tell you to the really dangerous violent criminal. They are not stereotypical. The good news is that you do not have to be stereotypical, either. Think deeply on this.

The gift of underestimation

Having been in hundreds of fights and literally several lethal force encounters, I can tell you that I am quite naturally a compulsive sandbagger. I will hide my capabilities even during a fight until I am ready to use them. I will bait my opponent into boldness and overconfidence, both before and during a confrontation. If they have chosen to make it go physical, and I cannot avoid it, then I still want to surprise them. The counter-ambush is so effective with concealment that it becomes an ambush itself by definition. How does the counter-ambush become the ambush? Concealment. The very definition of ambush is to use concealment and the element of surprise to attack. Of course, we know that the element of surprise is created by effective concealment. Therefore, if we can effectively conceal our capabilities and intent during an attack on us, we can counter with enough concealed force to completely take the attacker by surprise and wreck their entire confidence loop. This is the violence of mind principle at work. It is violence of action premeditated by preparation and orientation, violence of mind.

There have been many fights I have won or survived because I was sorely underestimated in some way. A few of those times I think they underestimated how fucking fast I could run! (Parkour has been a thing in the criminal world long before it hit YouTube. Joking, but not joking.) Humor aside, the awareness that concealment gives you the element of surprise, even during a fight, is a huge turning point for the violent person. It's that moment when you become seriously dangerous, bolder, and more confident in all capabilities and boundaries because you now have the *secret* weapons.

In prison, or anywhere where wolves congregate, it is widely known that the worst person to attack is the one who has repeatedly proven to be unpredictable. An attack is always predicated on an element of prediction. Overt deterrence projects predictability. Covert Deterrence projects unpredictability. If you cannot at least believe you can moderately predict the outcome, you will most likely not attack. The only effective way to deal with the truly unpredictable is through ambush execution, meaning the attacker is intent on assassination (to kill suddenly or secretly) with little to no chance of the victim fighting back. While it's easy to see why this can become a problem for the unpredictable fighter in prison or the hood, it's a testament to how effective it will be against a chance encounter attack on the streets.

Because I seek to blend in and not bring any attention to myself, concealment is my main weapon. Weaponize the surprise. But just because I may have to project my intent a little, such as when I am in those rougher areas, it does not mean that I am not still concealing many things from a potential attacker. Often that is the very idea that I am trying to convey by revealing just a little bit of that alpha energy. "You do not know what I am capable of, and this should give you caution if you are attached to your own well-being." In the end, an attacker underestimating you is always a gift. Effective concealment of your capabilities, weapons and intentions, before and throughout the fight, is how you win that gift.

Ambush and Counter-ambush

Ambush is defined, simply, as a *surprise attack from a position of concealment.* What most people do not understand is the word "concealment." It does not always mean lying hidden in the bushes. It often means concealing any threat or intentions of threat in order to get close enough to strike. In prison and in bad neighborhoods, one such method was to approach a target and ask, "Hey man, you got an extra cigarette?" That sentence is enough to work your way to within striking distance of the target. And with good concealment and emotional control, an attacker can render the target disarmed during the approach because they know that the target can't reasonably react to a threat that just isn't apparently there at all (exploitation of social courtesies). It is the easiest way to close distance, especially in public or other social settings where being approached in this way would be considered *normal* behavior.

For these types of attacks, preparation will include both deterrence and counter-ambush fight training. This would deal with everything from early recognition, posturing, decision making and positioning all the way to reflex-reaction training and clinch fighting. My "Gutter Fight" pistol class deals with this option in training, as does any of my training in the gym. The ability to respond faster than expected with more force than expected is what defines a counter-ambush in self-defense. The details of this are much greater than I can cover in this book, but the general concepts I presented in this paragraph are the basis of how it should be approached.

Nonetheless, there is more to defending against ambush than simply using the counter-ambush. One can actually *ambush the ambusher*, so to speak. The definition, a surprise attack from a position of concealment, is applicable in complete visibility. It does not have to happen from being physically concealed as a person. Just like there are high-order criminals, there are high-order fighters with morally just missions as well. Being savvy to the techniques and requirements of a predator, one can literally be a step ahead of an attacker in one quick movement or series of movements. The term *violence of action* comes into play, but only if it is driven by a completely dedicated *violence of mind.*

This particular level of action requires forethought and predictive vision. Without truly applying nearly everything I have discussed in this book, you cannot achieve this. In my own experience, it was actual experience that helped cultivate the ability. It's like a very real exhibition of unexpectedly "opening a can of whoop ass." The attacker presents the green light, and the defender unleashes an explosive, decisive and highly trained set of skills, techniques and procedures packaged within a level of viciousness and commitment that the attacker will be overwhelmed by. And by deeming the attacker as the embodiment of evil, you open up the ferocity of hate because you clearly hate that which is evil. Your empathy for your fellow humans, who are victimized and have their lives destroyed by evil such as this, will drive your commitment in stopping it. This is the mindset of meeting ambush with ambush.

With the mindset and orientation squared away, the physical part comes from training. No one skill, technique or procedure will work universally. You will need to read the situation, the level of attack, the weapons of the attacker, the environment, and many other factors to decide how to respond. This is why force-on-force training is mandatory. You cannot develop those capabilities without being put in those situations at least in a mock realistic way with open variables. A non-compliant attacker is a must. The use of simulated ammunition training weapons and/or impact resistant attacker suits are a requirement. You have to be able to feel what it is like to actually follow through with strikes and weapons.

It is absolutely necessary to cultivate the abilities and mindset of ambushing the ambusher, if you want to be prepared to deal with the truly violent attacker. My training has gravitated towards understanding and building these capabilities. Counting on all confrontations to be with the standard, lazy, dumb and unskilled criminal actually *will* get you *kilt in da streetz*.

We are all wolves now

By now it should be clear that I'm no fan of the "sheepdog" analogy. If we are going to follow this line of thought, let's think about the "wolf" that we are training to fight. In the wild, the only known natural predators of wolves are other wolves and human hunters. If we want to take this ridiculous analogy to the letter, then we must become the wolf or the hunter to become a natural predator of the wolf. Both the wolf and the hunter are made up by everything we have covered in terms of wide-band situational awareness, watchfulness, patience, self-control, and being mission-focused. When stalking prey, or in an unfamiliar area alone, neither the wolf nor the hunter go tromping through loudly without regard. They watch, move with a low signal, do not appear threatening prematurely. In fact, very few natural predators want to be seen when they are being predators.

Chest beating, loud talking, open carrying weapons; these are behaviors akin to how predators behave in the safety of their own pack. If they behaved this way on the hunt or in battle, they would go extinct rather quickly. Typically, it is a behavior to establish rank, or to attract a mate for breeding. Unfortunately, men seem to think this attracts women when most often the loneliest guys you meet are over-the-top with all of this. Women are intrigued by the strong predator, the watchful hungry eyes, keeping a distance, no need to demand respect because presence commands it, gently coaxing with a hint of danger telling her that if she can get inside of that she will be protected and safe, drawing her in at her own pace… There are many ways to accomplish this, but the strongest predators work in this way.

I've heard other instructors refer to waking up the natural predator in students. I like that thought, because it's true. I often tell people that if I am encountered with a truly bad guy someday, I guarantee that episode will be *wolf on wolf* violence. Once I was

206

accompanying a female friend through an alley in downtown Youngstown at night. She asked, "what if someone comes to rob us?" My response was, "what if I rob him?" Of course, I was using somewhat truthful humor to help ease worries. The point is, when I walk through a bad area, I am a predator. I have maimed other humans. I spent five years in prison. While it's no guarantee you won't be challenged, and it is an art in avoiding that while signaling that you are not an easy mark, I subtly send the signal that I am at the least a dangerous predator in this area right now. I see everything and everyone. I keep my principal (my companion) in my view at all times, pulling a slight rear security. I am physically fit with a strong posture. My demeanor is relaxed, and I may even be smiling, but my eyes are on fire.

Just because you don't come from the same world that he most likely does, it does not mean that *you* are not capable of being the wolf the same as the bad guy, with the same drive and capabilities to apply to your mission. We are not that different. We are both human. We both have the same base instincts, the same "tools" at our disposal. We are both genetically the same species. One is not a predator and the other a defender. Both are predators. We are the same, human beings. The only thing that separates us is the objective in our very different missions. In the end, we are both predators. Wake up and do your genetically determined job.

I also think it is a huge mistake to look at people like they are "sheep". First, it's degrading. You are being facetious or downright arrogant if you devalue people that you do not even know. Sheepdogs protect sheep who are used as livestock, bought and sold, and ultimately slaughtered. Is that your noble job? More importantly, remember the rule: stop looking *for* things and start looking *at* things. You will be looking for sheep, and not see *the wolves looking directly at you*. Trust me, you cannot assume that anyone is weak and harmless. Many of the men I met in prison were hard to read, and some were downright misleading. Some were charming, good looking, articulate. Others appeared weak and submissive, but were terribly dangerous as process predators such as rapists or serial killers. Stop being full of yourself and looking at yourself like you are some special breed; you are not. You have a value system that is possibly more honorable, but you are not above people you do not know anything about. Think that way, and you may find yourself physically beneath them one day.

CHAPTER TWELVE: DAILY CONSIDERATIONS

A knife is not a suitable self-defense weapon (for most of you)

Of course, it's well established that I have stabbed people. I have been cut and stabbed. I have endured not only the court system specifically over lethal force with a knife, but I also endured the prison system and dealt with the parole board over that first 4 years. I lived for 5 years inside of a system of brutality where edged weapons are the primary weapons. I don't care how long someone has "studied" a knife "art" you just cannot duplicate real experience with all of the complex issues that civilians face with knife violence. From the realities and the mechanics of how it really happens, to the aftermath and legal issues that drag on from it.

One of the most important things that is overlooked by nearly everyone who carries a knife for self-defense is that fact that there are not many cases where self-defense with a knife does not lead to criminal charges. We hear stories everyday about citizens who defend themselves with guns, and often are never charged. This means that police determined not to arrest them after the incident, and that the prosecutor further declined to press charges. It really has become socially acceptable to shoot someone with a gun in self-defense. This is not true of the knife. The knife is brutal. Savage. Incredibly bloody. You become the butcher of another human. It's up close and personal...

The perception of knife violence is one of brutality and extremism. Watch any number of available surveillance videos of people being stabbed. It takes numerous stab wounds before someone even slows down. What this means is that you will likely have to stab someone several times, and by several, I mean 15, 20 or 30, to get them to stop their attack on you. The incredible problem that this poses for you becomes clear the moment the police roll up and there you are, completely soaked in this guy's blood looking freaked the fuck out, and there he is, on the ground with an insane number of holes in him. Do you really, honestly believe that any rational cop is going to be like, "OK, we can see who's the good guy here. Go ahead home and wash all that blood off and we'll call you if we have any questions"? No. It doesn't happen like that. When that level of violence has been used, everyone goes to the station and the investigation starts. If the other guy is dead or unconscious, they are certainly not going to let a freaked out, blood-soaked knife wielder tell his version and then just go free. Are you serious? So, they'll charge you, hold you, and begin an investigation.

You just cannot cite knife defenses where the defender was not taken into custody and charged. If you find any at all, compare that with the frequency of how often it happens with firearms. The guys who do get off from knife defense cases only do so after enduring massive court proceedings, charges, and often trials. Which is where that other problem, the brutality perception, will beat you senseless. How do you stand and explain why any rational and peaceful person would stab another human being 15, 20 or 30 times? And you will have to explain this to people who have no idea what it takes to stop a human from violence, and how much the body can take before it drops. These are the same people that say things like, "Why didn't the cop just shoot him in the leg, or shoot the gun out of his hand?" When police have public shootings. What do you think they see a stabbing as? On TV, you stab someone once and they fall! They learned about violence from TV. "20 or 30 times is murderous hate and aggression", they'll say.

Let's not forget that whole thing about 95% of charges ending in plea bargains in the U.S. It's not an exact number, but I believe it's pretty damn accurate having been inside of the system myself for many years. We just are not at a point in history where the public perception of knife violence has anything good attached to it. It's a truth.

I bet your knife fighting self-defense guru didn't teach you any of that.

The type of knife DOES matter

When I was sentenced, I had a "tail" which meant that I could see a parole board to have hearings for possible early release. When I was sitting in my first parole hearing, about a year into my sentence, I endured the most brutal, degrading verbal attack I've ever had, and it was largely over my "intentions" for carrying a knife. Let me clarify, the knife I used in this particular case was a standard, old school cheap folder with a wooden handle and brass end pieces. It was probably purchased at a flea market for $5. In no way did this knife look threatening in any fighting sense, with its standard four-inch, non-serrated blade.

The parole board said things like, "Why were you even carrying a knife? You obviously wanted to stab someone if you were even carrying a knife!" I attempted to explain that carrying a pocket knife was something that all the men in my family did, as did all of the men I even knew. I explained that it was for utility, like working on cars, cutting hoses, opening boxes, etc. One parole board member said, in a most memorable mean tone, "My best friend is a car mechanic, and he doesn't use a pocket knife to work on cars, he doesn't carry a knife, your story is bullshit, and your intentions were clear when you carried that knife. If we could add time to your sentence we would, but for now we will deny you any chance at early release."

I will always remember this as one of those paradigm shifting moments in life where something that I thought was normal and benign was shown to be something that was used against me in a terrible, life altering way and I was powerless to change it. For a moment, just imagine if the knife I had used was "tactical" or some sort of fighting pick. I shudder inside at that thought, after what I went through over carrying a boring, dull old timer. Choose your weapons and carry implements wisely based on the perception of those who will judge you, not what you "think" or your personal perception of your choices.

"KNIFE DEFENSE" TRAINING

This is where I also, with no apology, part ways with the "self-defense" community. The first and foremost problem about knife defense is that -nearly- no one teaching it really knows how to defend against a knife because they have never defended against a knife. Period. Yes, this includes people who "say" they have been in "knife fights" in their classes, but there are no scars, no prison records, etc. I have yet to walk into a "knife defense" class and see someone teaching something that I think would even remotely work, given the number of stabbings I have personally participated in.

Knives are scary, deadly. Truly violent people are scary, deadly. I will say in all honesty that the average person truly has little chance against a surprise knife attack. If we don't face that fact, we can't work to gain the advantages that remove "average" and "surprise" out of that equation. It's just a fucking fact. I've seen it in action against strong guys, and I've used it. It's a terrible weapon to defend against. You have basically three main procedural goals in a close knife defense:

1. Work to limit his force production
2. Work to limit his targets (you choose where you get cut, because you WILL get cut)
3. Work towards an ultimate solution via time bought with #1 and #2 and end the problem for a permanent result.

The principle objectives of those goals are to limit force production and limit target areas, especially by protecting critical areas. The biggest mistake I have seen stabbing victims make (and yes, I have seen many stabbings and have stabbed people, and have been stabbed) is that they do not protect vital areas because they are just worried about getting stabbed and try to reflexively cover up and deflect. That does not work with a knife. It takes a great deal of courage to accept that you will be cut and accept it enough to actively work to limit what areas you will be cut in, while simultaneously taking cuts to the arm, etc.

This is a level of courage most people's brains are not ready to process. There's a point in every stabbing we called "the quit" where the victim is overwhelmed and gives up to die (or in the irrational hope that the attacker will stop). I have watched this happen in a man's eyes as I repeatedly stabbed him, he went into a very relaxed state, slid backwards onto the floor, bleeding out, and said "I'm sorry". I've watched it happen to other men, strong men and predators alike, on the concrete floors of prison bathrooms and card rooms.

Whether it's from physiological shock, or psychological shock, doesn't matter. This moment comes, and it comes quick, and the predator is acutely aware of that moment because it is the moment of total control. TOTAL control over that human being. When a predator achieves "the quit" in its prey, at least once, then they know that is what they are working towards. This changes the game for them. The fierceness of the attack, showing them their own blood, talking to them, all of these things can speed up "the quit". When someone is being stabbed and the attacker is telling them they are going to die, it has an unbelievable effect on the victim. The defender, who has been taught by inexperienced people, has no idea about this endgame, the different ways it's achieved and how quickly it happens. There is no mindset work behind the "techniques" shown to them.

KNIFE "FIGHTING"

Prison knifing is a style of killing with an edged weapon that is generations upon generations old with an unbroken lineage of development to this day. Through direct experience, and lessons passed on, this style has been refined and honed within a system of simplicity. I want you to think about this for a moment, as this is one of those beautiful examples life gives us of something very real to learn from.

Prison knife fighting is probably the *purest lineage* of pure knife aggression in existence. It is undoubtedly the "style" with the most kills. As a style that has been developed through real predator-on-predator attacks, the necessity for efficiency is extremely high due to the dangerous nature of most intended targets. This produces a system of efficiency and effectiveness with absolutely no flash or frills. This is often a very strong indicator of a style's application and origins: how simple and efficient the tasks are within the style. Necessity has created the simple and fast system of attack in the prison knife world because it is simply too dangerous to have a fight dragged out in length. Some of the dangers are:

- The intended victim can fight back and even counter-attack with a shank (knife) of his own, and if given a chance he is likely to be a formidable opponent
- The victim's friends or fellow gang members can become activated and aid in the fight against the attacker
- The guards can come at any time and stop the attack before the victim's fate is sealed, this poses a few problems in itself:
  - The guards will lock up the attacker in solitary, and probably will charge the attacker with more crimes and further prison time
  - The victim may be saved and will return for blood one day, so the attacker will have to live in watch 24/7

So, let's examine some of the elements at play in this system. Time and efficiency are obviously very important elements on the list of underlying principles, as outlined earlier. But what else can we learn from it? While I have had the privilege of participating in and witnessing first-hand these types of fights, you still have the opportunity to view them via surveillance videos on the internet. I encourage you to do just that; find as many prison stabbing videos as you can and study all of them. The primary objective seems to be to put as many deep holes as possible into vital areas as quickly as possible.

I recently read a news story about a stabbing in a halfway house (pre-release center for convicts where they are "supervised" but can go into society unsupervised). The fight started over an argument about a football game, the stabbing victim punched the other guy over the argument, and subsequently he was stabbed to death. Here is the breakdown: 90 stab wounds, 5 to the heart, 1 to the carotid artery, and 1 to the brain. Multiple critical hits were achieved by using the "sewing machine" method to *saturate* the opening with wounds. (Over something like a football game.) It's literally the fastest and most effective way to shorten the victim's time of being functional.

Prison stabbings are plentiful; they happen very frequently. In most of those stabbings the number of wounds in the victim numbers into the dozens. While much of that is a psychological message to others (and an exercise of letting the beast inside run free), it's worth mentioning again that it typically takes a lot of knife wounds to stop a dedicated attacker.

Looking at it from a pragmatic perspective, the slashy, fancy art of "knife fighting systems" would actually create way more wounds which would fail to stop the person, requiring even more wounds. This might work on someone who was not intent on attacking and who can clearly see they are getting cut causing them to make the decision to stop. However, it just would not stand up in the pressure testing of a prison atmosphere. This is my opinion, the opinion of someone who has stabbed people, has been stabbed, and has watched people get stabbed, both on the streets and in prison.

An example of a psychological stoppage would be when an adolescent friend got stabbed when we were teenagers. We got into a little bit of shit with some random guys, and during the fight one of them stabbed John in the kidney one time. John quit fighting, and the guy quit stabbing. But this is more common in social violence where the goal is to kick someone's ass and teach them a lesson, not in violence where someone wants to eliminate you for whatever reason. The reality is typically a lot messier and people often don't even realize they are being stabbed until you are well into a dozen wounds. You have to explain this to a court system/society that does not understand this. Think about that the next time you strap on that fancy fighting knife for your EDC badassery.

ETIQUETTE: THE "CEREMONY OF RESPECT" IN VIOLENCE CULTURE

Self-control must be practiced outside of violence and training for it to be real in your life and your skill sets. From the samurai to the knighthood, politeness, character, self-control and loyalty have been standards in warrior code of conduct for thousands of years. For good reasons, it has long been considered the pinnacle of warriorhood to be able to set down the implements and language of war, don your best sword (or concealed Glock) and attend social events displaying impeccable behavior and hospitality. To be generous with friends and associates, and courteous and protective with the ladies, was an exhibition of a self-actualized warrior; to have *savage on-tap*, yet be exquisite and sharp in public. This became the mark of success in both the personal and professional lives of warriors in nearly every civilized culture. It also allowed the fighter to fit into whatever environment he found himself in, the ability to operate across classes effectively.

What does this have to do with violence in today's world? Everything. If you believe anything I talked about in this book, you will see how your daily conduct in non-fighting activities is the manifestation of your orientation and conditioning. I have said for many years that people, unless they have been trained otherwise, will always fight the same way that they communicate. Quick to anger in talks equals quick to anger in fights, and so on. It is more befitting of a warrior to be confident, calm, watchful, thoughtful, well-liked and popular, strong in appearance without boasting or working hard to appear strong, polite, and in good physical condition. These are all results of proper training, conditioning, orientation and self-control, and will naturally emerge if you properly train and groom yourself for *defensive* fighting.

Avoidance, mindset, situational awareness, diplomacy, self-control, strength, values; these are all emphasized as being critical elements in your preparation for violence, yet we too often overlook them in true daily practice. How do you expect to perform something under a rare demand, when you simply do not practice it daily? Surely you can see the connections between mindfulness practices in fighting and mindfulness practices in daily activities. Knowing how mindfulness practices, such as awareness and self-control, can help one avoid or win a fight, why would you not aspire to practice them at all times?

This is what I mean when I say people pay lip-service to the topics of mindset and self-control. They *say* it's important, but then act like it's only something they need to practice in the gym, or on the range, because they will only need it in a fight. The reality is that *you will not successfully perform that self-control if you do not practice it daily.*

Self-control is such a monumental undertaking that you simply cannot master yourself without constant effort; the more you engage in that forces you to practice it, the better. This can be the discipline to make time for others who have traveled to your area, or it can be the self-control to not stare at a woman's breasts when she is attempting to do business with you or just trying enjoy your company socially. Seriously. Every opportunity to practice self-control cultivates that mindset and it WILL carry over into your fighting.

For the purpose here in this book, I want to isolate this self-control concept within a fighting/violence framework. However, I will briefly mention two things here. First, I acknowledge that the trained and skilled can often deceive any reliable read on their capabilities. I still contend that you can glean the information needed from this behavior as well, but that is for a more in-depth discussion.

Next, one may not be accomplished in this in all company. What I mean here is that there may be certain people or groups of people that will trigger involuntary emotional responses in you (or someone you are trying to read). This is why I am emphasizing that self-control needs practiced *always*, and not just on the range, on the mat, or out in public. If you can find breaks in your ability to maintain control (arguments from an ex, or family, for example) then you have found a deficiency, a weakness, in your ability to control yourself overall. The reason you will fight the way you communicate is because *you are who you practice being*. Not who you think you are, and not who you appear to be on the range or on the mat, but who you actually are, 24 hours a day, 7 days a week. You will fight, communicate, date, love and do business the way you do because you are who you practice being all day.

DO UNTO OTHERS…

You cannot get very far in life without the cooperation of others. Life is about communication. Whether the communicating is done through sharing, monetary exchange, or force, we must interact. Be strong. If you cannot look a strong man in the eye and shake his hand, or go into negotiations with him, how can you think you will have the confidence to face a strong man who is trying to kill you? Men, treat women with respect. One of the biggest tells I have found in the business world about how a guy will be to do business with is how he treats and views other people, especially women. If he is rotten about it and apparently looks down on employees or women, he will eventually look down on you or your associates, too, because he is pre-dispositioned to devalue others to over-value himself. Women are simply the easiest target, so he picks them first. Treat people with respect and interact politely with people who do the same.

It's important here to discuss toxic people. There is a nuance in the "do onto others" rule that has to do with breaking ties with people who are not beneficial to be involved with. Nothing says that every relationship will be a good one, or one that is mutually beneficial. Some will position themselves in your life or operations in ways that they were not invited. Or they will gain those positions through deception or upfront generosity that will later come with a price. Some people have personal issues or hidden agendas, and sometimes relationships just change with time. The worst ones will eventually leverage themselves against your attempts to be in control of yourself.

What I mean is, at some point it will become evident that it is not in your best interest to be involved with them any longer. At this moment, they may attack you with your own code of conduct and say, "You *must* treat me well, you profess to be professional and polite and I *demand* that you treat me this way!" They will use your obvious manners and courtesy against you. It is never acceptable to allow someone to put you down, or to take credit for your hard work. If you choose to cut ties with someone, my suggestion is to be firm and polite, and be prepared for a storm of emotional outbursts and possibly public backlash. The important thing is to not allow it to break your own code of conduct. The manipulative person will attack in a way specifically to get you to break that conduct so they can point out "bad" behavior to justify themselves.

Your reputation is a product of your conduct and of the company you allow to represent your "brand" through friendships and business associations. Always keep this in mind. The professional knows when to cut ties and also how to accept losses for future gain. Let people act how they wish, without allowing it to change your personal behavior. Learning how to both read people accurately and how to establish and protect your own boundaries will go a long way toward minimizing your contact with such people. This is important because it applies in violence and combat as well. Danger does not always come in the form of recognizable danger. Avoidance and evasion should be practiced socially if you wish to effectively avoid or evade violent encounters someday.

Behaving well with self-control and generosity is a ceremony of respect; a respect for the value of knowing others, of spending time with them. Remember, those of us who have participated in extreme violence, who have watched friends and family leave this earth, know the value of friendships and the people we like. Friendships become more meaningful. Potential friendships become more meaningful. Potential dangers become more meaningful. Time becomes precious. Business and success are tied to communication and value-based judgement. To devalue such things is the mark of an amateur, in both personal interactions and in combat.

This will keep you out of trouble while building your watchfulness and self-control. It is an exhibition of taking the concepts of awareness, avoidance, violence and relationships and taking them seriously by doing more than just paying lip service to them. This is a manifestation of strength in orientation and conditioning that happens every day in every situation, not just on the mat or on the range. To do otherwise is to just be self-absorbed and you will, no matter your credentials and experience level, fall into your own version of Dunning-Kruger. If you are too busy drinking your own cool-aid, you don't know half as much as you think you do about who is even in your presence and what is going on around you. Whether you want to be a tough guy, a "warrior", or just a successful and well-liked person, this is a good place to start.

You *are what you think*, not *what you think you are*

It's been said repeatedly by many great thinkers and successful people: You become what you think about. This does not mean that you become what you think you are. Many people in our sphere of the self-defense world fashion themselves to be warriors in their own mind. They train with weapons, go to the gym, spend countless hours on forums and social media learning and/or defending the almighty knowledge of warriorhood. The problem is, they spend so much time trying to be a warrior that they forget why they are doing it in the first place.

Most *profess* to practice self-defense because they want to save the lives of their loved ones as well as their own lives someday. It is presumed that the reason they want to preserve these lives is to enjoy their time on this earth with their loved ones. Instead of doing so, they spend every waking hour obsessing over guns, martial arts styles, techniques, training, politics of self-defense, and every other aspect of violence they can engage in on social media. Even if they spend some time with their family, they undoubtedly waste more time than they could count being a part of this "community".

Why are you not enjoying your time living the life that you profess to protect so viciously? Don't become obsessed with violence or the implements of it. It is an aspect of our existence that is inescapable. Yes, you should be prepared to face it and bring the heat like a lion defending its familial pride. But that does not mean you should forget to enjoy this life and enjoy the precious little time you have with your children, your spouse, your family. Play outside, go on vacations, spend couch time with them. Touch your wife's hair, play in your child's world with them. Spend your time making the memories that will calm your soul on the day that you face your death.

The internet can live without your two cents about guns, gear, techniques and who is legitimate and who isn't. And trust me, while it's important to teach family the basic tenets of self-defense and awareness, your family does not need to hear about how fucking scary the world is 24 hours a day from you. That will not make them any safer, and in fact will stress them out and probably make them despise the whole thing you love so much. Don't be a source of stress to them. Stop loving your (inexperienced) idea of violence. Love your family, practice strength and self-control, and it won't be a problem.

Violence ruins lives. It changes things forever. It can take away loved ones, freedom, opportunities...changes that last a lifetime and oftentimes from which there can be no recovery, *ever*. Some of us know this all too well. Be ready, but don't glorify it in your mind. Practice the things I have talked about in this book, and focus on living a strong, happy, productive, and protected life.

This book is full of useless information

The last thing I will say is that this book, which you are now finished reading, is full of useless information. Completely worthless.

There is a second component that must be added to it to make it have any meaning or be worth anything to you at all. You see, knowledge alone is just potential. Potential that is never used is absolutely worthless. Execution is knowledge manifested, and it is knowledge gained and evolved. Make this information worth something. Formulate a plan and *execute on that plan every single day*.

That is how you win.

Varg Freeborn

Made in the USA
Lexington, KY
04 March 2019